D1584857

INTELLECTUAL PROPERTY LAW

Visit the *Law Express Series* Companion Website at **www.pearsoned.co.uk/lawexpress** to find valuable **student** learning material including:

■ A study plan test to assess how well you know the subject before you begin your revision, now broken down into targeted study units

■ Interactive quizzes with a variety of question types to test your knowledge of the main points from each chapter of the book

■ Further examination questions and guidelines for answering them

■ Interactive flashcards to help you revise the main terms and cases

■ Printable versions of the topic maps and checklists

Plus:

■ 'You be the marker' allows you to see exam questions and answers from the perspective of the examiner and includes notes on how an answer might be marked

■ Podcasts provide point-by-point instruction on how to answer a common exam question

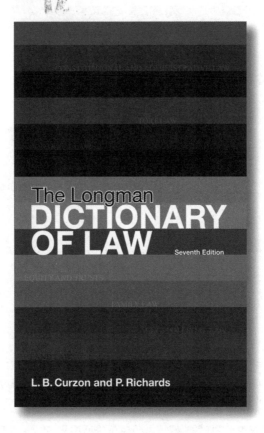

Law Express

INTELLECTUAL PROPERTY LAW

Professor David Bainbridge
Claire Howell

PEARSON

Longman

Harlow, England • London • New York • Boston • San Francisco • Toronto • Sydney • Singapore • Hong Kong
Tokyo • Seoul • Taipei • New Delhi • Cape Town • Madrid • Mexico City • Amsterdam • Munich • Paris • Milan

Pearson Education Limited
Edinburgh Gate
Harlow
Essex CM20 2JE
England

and Associated Companies throughout the world

Visit us on the World Wide Web at:
www.pearsoned.co.uk

First published 2009

ISBN: 978-1-4058-5954-7

British Library Cataloguing-in-Publication Data
A catalogue record for this book is available from the British Library

Library of Congress Cataloging-in-Publication Data
Bainbridge, David I.
   Intellectual property law / David Bainbridge, Claire Howell. -- 1st ed.
       p. cm.
   Includes bibliographical references and index.
   ISBN 978-1-4058-5954-7 (pbk. : alk. paper) 1. Intellectual property--Great
Britain. I. Howell, Claire. II. Title.
   KD1269.B356 2009
   346.4104'8--dc22

                                        2008027600

10 9 8 7 6 5 4 3 2 1
12 11 10 09 08

Typeset in 10pt Helvetica Condensed by 3
Printed and bound in Great Britain by Henry Ling Ltd, Dorchester, Dorset

Contents

Supporting resources

Visit the *Law Express Series* Companion Website at **www.pearsoned.co.uk/lawexpress** to find valuable student learning material.

Companion Website for students
- A study plan test to assess how well you know the subject before you begin your revision, now broken down into targeted study units
- Interactive quizzes with a variety of question types to test your knowledge of the main points from each chapter of the book
- Further examination questions and guidelines for answering them
- Interactive flashcards to help you revise the main terms and cases
- Printable versions of the topic maps and checklists
- 'You be the marker' allows you to see exam questions and answers from the perspective of the examiner and includes notes on how an answer might be marked
- Podcasts provide point-by-point instruction on how to answer a common exam question

Also: The Companion Website provides the following features:

- Search tool to help locate specific items of content
- E-mail results and profile tools to send results of quizzes to instructors
- Online help and support to assist with website usage and troubleshooting

For more information please contact your local Pearson Education sales representative or visit **www.pearsoned.co.uk/lawexpress**

Acknowledgements

Publisher's acknowledgements

Our thanks go to all reviewers who contributed to the development of this text, including students who participated in research and focus groups which helped to shape the series format.

Introduction

Intellectual property law is a demanding but enjoyable subject. It covers a range of rights, some of which have little in common with others. Students should keep in mind that, although some rights may be quite different from others, a number of rights may exist in respect of the same subject-matter. For example, a new design of plastic bottle for tomato ketchup may be protected by design law (registered and unregistered), trade mark law and the law of passing off. The label attached to the bottle may be protected by artistic and literary copyright. Students are likely to get extra marks if they can demonstrate that they understand the overlap between the different intellectual property rights.

This book is a revision guide. It is intended to help focus students on the key areas in which they are likely to be examined. It also acts as an aide memoire, picking out key cases and statutes. It is no substitute for textbooks and other materials with which students should be familiar. Students should also be aware that this revision guide cannot cover all the ground which may be covered in a module on intellectual property. For example, it has not been possible to cover areas such as the database right (students should be familiar with the important *British Horseracing Board* v *William Hill* case) or rights in performances.

Students should frequently check the syllabus of the module they are taking and refer to lecture notes, handouts and virtual learning materials provided by their lecturer and module leader. As intellectual property is such a big subject, most lecturers are likely to concentrate on some parts of the subject and deal with others in less detail. By reviewing the content of the course as taught or given as directed learning, students will have a much better idea of the areas they are likely to be examined on. Past examination papers also provide a rich form of guidance but students must be aware that, in a fast moving subject like intellectual property, older examination questions may have been overtaken by recent developments.

It is certainly worthwhile attempting questions in past examination papers but, if not sure about the current relevance of particular questions, students should consult their lecturers if there is any doubt about this. Ideally, students should attempt past examination questions after getting to grips with the subject area. Allow the time permitted in the examination and go through the answer afterwards critically, seeing how the answer could be improved.

Inevitably, during the teaching of a module, there will be legislative changes to and/or important cases on intellectual property law. Examiners are impressed with students who show that they have taken the trouble to look up and understand the latest developments. Students should also be reminded that it is well worth reading the judgments in important House of Lords, Court of Appeal and European Court of Justice cases on intellectual property. Taking the trouble to read judgments and other materials such as journal articles will usually reward the student by giving him or her a deeper understanding of the subject.

REVISION NOTES

Things to bear in mind when revising Intellectual Property Law:

- Problem questions can be quite complex and it might be worthwhile drawing a 'mind map' or making a list of relevant dates before attempting the question. Spend a little time ensuring you understand the question.
- Essay questions often require students to consider policy issues or unsatisfactory areas such as software patents.
- Exam questions are not an excuse to write down everything you know about a particular area – answer what the question asks, not what you wish it had asked.
- Make full use of the recommended textbooks and other materials your lecturer suggests. **Do not rely on this revision guide to learn the subject**.
- Make sure you understand the main legislative provisions dealing with matters such as subsistence, requirements for registration, authors, designers and inventors, ownership and entitlement, duration, infringement and defences.
- Seek advice from your lecturer about what you should revise. Most lecturers are very happy to give advice, guidance and feedback.
- Do not 'cherry-pick', only revising part of the syllabus. Questions on intellectual property often cover a wide range and may include a number of different intellectual property rights. Only omit revising a particular part of the syllabus if your lecturer has expressly confirmed it will not be examined.
- Attempt past examination questions and review how your answer could be improved. Some lecturers are happy to look at your attempts and to give you feedback. But make sure you do not waste time attempting past questions that are no longer relevant because of changes in the law.

Guided Tour

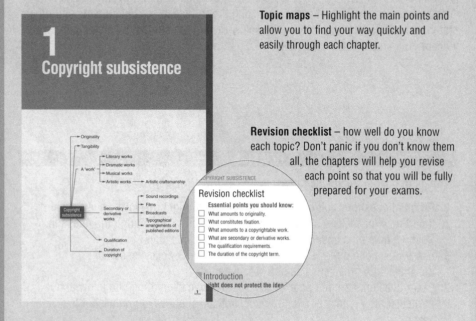

Topic maps – Highlight the main points and allow you to find your way quickly and easily through each chapter.

Revision checklist – how well do you know each topic? Don't panic if you don't know them all, the chapters will help you revise each point so that you will be fully prepared for your exams.

Sample questions – Prepare for what you will be faced with in your exams! Guidance on structuring strong answers is provided at the end of the chapter.

Sample question

Could you answer this question? Below is a typical essay question that could arise on this topic. Guidelines on answering the question are included at the end of this chapter, whilst a sample problem question and guidance on tackling it can be found on the companion website.

Key definition boxes – Make sure you understand essential legal terms.

KEY DEFINITION
Original. The work has originated from the author and has not been copied from another work.

Problem area – Highlight areas where students most often trip up in exams. Use them to make sure you do not make the same mistakes.

Problem area: fixation by another

It does seem difficult to understand that fixation can be made even without the knowledge or licence of the author of the 'work'. Make sure however that you do not confuse the situation of a secretary taking dictation, where they will not obtain copyright in the written work, and the reporter in *Walter v Lane*. Due to the reporter expending extra skills in the reporting of the speech, copyright vested both in the

Key case and key statute boxes – Identify the essential cases and statutes that you need to know for your exams.

KEY CASE

Interlego AG v Tyco Indus

Concerning: whether small 'Lego' bricks gave rise to a

Facts

The original Lego bricks had these had expired. Some ch later bricks were being co

Legal principle

KEY STATUTE

Section 3(2) and (3) Copyright, Designs and Patents Act 1988

Copyright does not subsist in a literary, dramatic or musical work unless and until it is recorded in writing or in any other way. It is immaterial whether the work is recorded by or with the permission of the author.

Further thinking box – Illustrates areas of academic debate, and point you towards that extra reading required for the top grades.

FURTHER THINKING

The distinction between interpretation and composition is a difficult one to make. For a clear summary of the problems associated with musicologists working on old material and whether what they are doing amounts to authorship or editing, see Peter Groves, 'Better than it sounds: originality of musical works' [2005] Ent LR 20.

Glossary – forgotten the meaning of a word? Where a word is highlighted in the text, turn to the glossary at the back of the book to remind yourself of its meaning.

Glossary of terms

The glossary is divided into two parts: **key definitions** and **other useful terms**.

The **key definitions** can be found within the chapter in which they occur as well as at the end of the book. These definitions are the essential terms that you must know and understand in order to prepare for an exam.

The additional list, **other useful terms**, provides further definitions of useful terms and phrases which will also help you answer examination and coursework questions effectively. These terms are highlighted in the text on their first occurrence but the definition can only be found here.

Exam tips – Want to impress examiners? These indicate how you can improve your exam performance and your chances of getting top marks.

EXAM TIP

Show an awareness of the practical consequences of copyright protection by pointing out that the failure to grant copyright for a single word is not just due to the *de minimis* principle. The intention in *Exxon* was to obtain greater protection over a range of goods via copyright than mere registration as a trade mark would have provided. There is also a public interest in preventing the control of words or phrases that should be available for all to use without fear of copyright infringement.

Revision notes – Highlight points that you should be aware of in other topic areas, or where your course may adopt a specific approach that you should check with your course tutor before reading further.

REVISION NOTE

Even though many of these more industrial works will fail to be classed as works of artistic craftsmanship they may be protected either as UK or Community registered designs or under the unregistered design right. See Chapter 7.

Guided tour of the companion website

 Book resources are available to download. Print your own **topic maps** and **revision checklists!**

 Use the **study plan** prior to your revision to help you assess how well you know the subject and determine which areas need most attention. Choose to take the full assessment or focus on targeted study units.

 'Test your knowledge' of individual areas with quizzes tailored specifically to each chapter. A variety of multiple choice, true and false and fill-in-the-blank question types ensure you are prepared for anything. Sample problem and essay questions are also available with guidance on crafting a good answer.

 Flashcards help improve recall of important legal terms and key cases. Use online, print for a handy reference or download to iPod for on-the-go revision!

'**You be the marker**' gives you the chance to evaluate sample exam answers for different question types and understand how and why an examiner awards marks.

Download the **podcast** and listen as your own personal Law Express tutor guides you through a 10-15 minute audio session. You will be presented with a typical but challenging question and provided a step-by-step explanation on how to approach the question, what essential elements your answer will need for a pass, how to structure a good response, and what to do to make your answer stand out so that you can earn extra marks.

All of this and more can be found when you visit
www.pearsoned.co.uk/lawexpress

Table of cases, statutes, statutory instruments and European Community legislation

Cases

Statutes

Statutory instruments

European Community Legislation

Conventions

1

Copyright subsistence

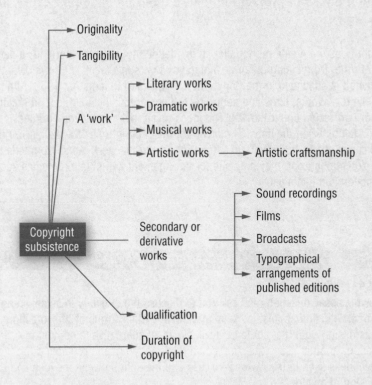

- Originality
- Tangibility
- A 'work'
  - Literary works
  - Dramatic works
  - Musical works
  - Artistic works → Artistic craftsmanship
- Copyright subsistence
  - Secondary or derivative works
    - Sound recordings
    - Films
    - Broadcasts
    - Typographical arrangements of published editions
  - Qualification
  - Duration of copyright

A printable version of this topic map is available from www.pearsoned.co.uk/lawexpress

Revision checklist

Essential points you should know:

- [ ] What amounts to originality.
- [ ] What constitutes fixation.
- [ ] What amounts to a copyrightable work.
- [ ] What are secondary or derivative works.
- [ ] The qualification requirements.
- [ ] The duration of the copyright term.

Introduction

Copyright does not protect the idea but the independent expression of the idea.

Copyright does not create monopolies. It is intended to prevent others, for a defined period of time, from taking unfair advantage of a person's creative efforts. What will be protected is stipulated in the Copyright, Designs and Patents Act 1988. Although original literary works, films and sound recordings are all included, not all creative efforts are protected under the Act. This does mean that some highly original creations fall between the lines. The owner of the copyright has the exclusive right to do, or licence others to do, certain acts in relation to the work. Apart from where certain exceptions exist, they may sue for infringement and obtain remedies such as an injunction and damages.

Assessment advice

Essay questions

A possible essay question may ask you to discuss the difficulty in establishing a work of artistic craftsmanship. Keep in mind any other forms of IP protection such as design right that could be available as an alternative to copyright protection. Another essay question could relate to the gap in protection for creative ideas seen in the *Norowzian* case and the split between the idea and the expression of a work.

Assessment advice

Problem questions

A problem question could include a scenario where a work is put into tangible form by another, where there is a trivial or *de minimis* work or a work with no artistic merit. There may also be an issue raised relating to sound recordings including qualification and duration issues on both derivative and original works.

Sample question

Could you answer this question? Below is a typical essay question that could arise on this topic. Guidelines on answering the question are included at the end of this chapter, whilst a sample problem question and guidance on tackling it can be found on the companion website.

ESSAY QUESTION

The formats of television game shows and reality programmes, such as *Pop Idol* and *Big Brother*, are inadequately protected by copyright in the UK. The time is right to introduce format rights as a new type of copyright work.
  Discuss with reference to decided cases.

■ Originality

Not all creative effort is protected. For protection the output must fall into the category of 'works' and must be original.

KEY STATUTE

Section 1 Copyright, Designs and Patents Act 1988

A property right subsists in original literary, dramatic, musical and artistic works as well as sound recordings, films, broadcasts and typographical arrangements of published editions.

KEY DEFINITION

Original. The work has originated from the author and has not been copied from another work.

Originality for copyright purposes does not demand the novelty or innovation required in order to obtain a patent. For copyright, original means that the work originated from the author its creator, it has not been copied from another's work. This is a very low but minimum standard. A one-line drawing would be regarded as too trivial to merit copyright protection.

Interlego AG v Tyco Industries Inc [1989] 1 AC 217, HL

Concerning: whether small modifications made to existing drawings of 'Lego' bricks gave rise to a fresh copyright

Facts

The original Lego bricks had had a patent and were registered as a design but these had expired. Some changes had been made to the design and these later bricks were being copied by Tyco. Lego claimed copyright infringement.

Legal principle

For copyright to exist there must be an original work. Even though modifications are technically significant, if they are not visually significant they would not give rise to a new copyright.

To hold otherwise would result in the possibility that copyright, in what was essentially the same work, could be extended indefinitely by merely making minor changes. Facts are not protected and a name such as Exxon cannot be subject to copyright even if a lot of work has gone into its creation. However, it has been held that headlines on an internet website could be a literary work.

EXAM TIP

Show an awareness of the practical consequences of copyright protection by pointing out that the failure to grant copyright for a single word is not just due to the *de minimis* principle. The intention in *Exxon* was to obtain greater protection over a range of goods via copyright than mere registration as a trade mark would have provided. There is also a public interest in preventing the control of words or phrases that should be available for all to use without fear of copyright infringement.

■ Tangibility

Copyright does not protect ideas, only a particular expression of an idea. Artistic works will usually be in tangible form, otherwise they could not be seen, but they do need some sort of surface to exist upon. In order to protect an idea in a literary, dramatic or musical work the expression must be recorded in a permanent form.

This can be in writing or in any other way. All new methods of recording or fixation are covered in the Act.

Section 3(2) and (3) Copyright, Designs and Patents Act 1988

Copyright does not subsist in a literary, dramatic or musical work unless and until it is recorded in writing or any other way. It is immaterial whether the work is recorded by or with the permission of the author.

There will be no copyright in an impromptu speech or a tune devised while playing the guitar unless they are recorded. The recording can be made by anyone, even without the permission of the author. On recording, fixation will take place and copyright will spring into existence.

REVISION NOTE

Who is the first owner of the copyright will be determined by who is the author of the work. Please refer to Chapter 2 on authorship and ownership.

Walter v *Lane* [1900] AC 539, HL

Concerning: the existence of copyright in an impromptu speech

Facts

The Earl of Rosebery made a speech. A reporter for *The Times* recorded it verbatim in shorthand, adding nothing apart from his reporting skills. The speech was published in *The Times* and copied by another. The issue was whether *The Times* had a right to sue for infringement.

Legal principle

The speaker was the author of the written work for copyright purposes. The reporter, having used skill and judgment in recording the speech, adding structure and punctuation, was the author of that report of the speech.

If the reporter had taped the speech on a tape machine he would have had copyright in the sound recording.

Problem area: Fixation by another

It does seem difficult to understand that fixation can be made even without the knowledge or licence of the author of the 'work'. Make sure however that you do not confuse the situation of a secretary taking dictation, where they will not obtain copyright in the written work, and the reporter in *Walter* v *Lane*. Due to the reporter expending extra skills in the reporting of the speech, copyright vested both in the author the Earl, and the reporter. If the reporter had only taken down some ideas expressed in the speech there would have been no fixation of the expression of Lord Rosebery.

■ A 'work'

The Act is very specific about what can be protected.

Literary works

KEY STATUTE

Section 3(1) Copyright, Designs and Patents Act 1988

A literary work is any work, other than a dramatic or musical work, which is written, spoken or sung, and includes a table or compilation (other than a database), a computer program, preparatory design material for a computer program and a database.

'Literary work' covers a work which is expressed in print or writing, irrespective of its quality. No merit is required. Compilations of literary works are protected but only if they are written. There is no protection for compilations of drawings.

Dramatic works

KEY STATUTE

Section 3(1) Copyright, Designs and Patents Act 1988

'A "dramatic" work includes a work of dance or mime.'

The dialogue of a dramatic work on its own is protected by literary copyright. A work of mime without words can be protected as a dramatic work. But there can be problems with outputs that do not fit the criteria of 'work'.

KEY CASE

Norowzian v *Arks Ltd* [2000] FSR 363, CA

Concerning: What constitutes a dramatic work

Facts

Mr Norowzian made the film *Joy*. It showed a man dancing and used 'flash framing' and 'jump cutting' (removing bits of film). Due to these editing techniques the dancing looked surreal. The man was doing things that in real time he could not have performed before an audience, hence this was not a dramatic work and was incapable of copyright protection.

Legal principle

The content of the film can be a dramatic work if it is '*a work of action with or without words or music which is capable of being performed before an audience*'. A film itself can be a work of action and be performed before an audience.

A film is a dramatic work distinct from the script. Rhythm, pace and movement are ideas, and cannot be protected as only the specific expression of the idea is covered. A similar problem of 'slipping through the net' is found in TV game-show formats. Often these comprise stock phrases or events which are interjected at appropriate times. For copyright to arise there must be fixation, a script recorded in permanent form. This is not appropriate to game-shows, which are expected to be spontaneous.

Problem area: This leaves a gap

If the purpose of copyright is to protect creative effort, it is not doing so. By being so prescriptive in what is a 'work', UK copyright law is failing to provide protection for creativity.

Musical works

For copyright purposes music and lyrics are separate. Lyrics are protected as literary works, so what is left is the music. The copyright can be owned by different people and expire at different times.

KEY STATUTE

Section 3(1) Copyright, Designs and Patents Act 1988

'A musical work is one consisting of music, exclusive of any words or action intended to be sung, spoken or performed with the music.'

There is, as with most of the other 'original' works, no quality requirement, and even a few notes may attract copyright. They must however be original. They may still be regarded as original musical works even if they are based on an existing piece of music. Such adaptations or transcriptions will attract their own copyright if the minimum amount of skill and labour has gone into their creation. It may be found however that the adaptation or transcription is infringing the copyright in the earlier musical work if made without the permission of the owner.

KEY CASE

Hyperion Records Ltd v *Sawkins* [2005] RPC 808, CA

Concerning: Whether a new copyright had been created by substantial editing

Facts

Dr Sawkins wrote new performing editions of some musical compositions that had gone out of copyright. He added some new aspects and changed some notes to make them possible to play. Hyperion rerecorded the music without the permission of Dr Sawkins, claiming that there was no copyright as it had expired. They were found to be infringing Sawkins's copyright.

Legal principle

This was not merely transcription. The notes are not the only expression that is protected by copyright. Other elements contribute to the sound of the music when performed and they can be protected if they are the product of an author's effort, skill and time.

FURTHER THINKING

The distinction between interpretation and composition is a difficult one to make. For a clear summary of the problems associated with musicologists working on old material and whether what they are doing amounts to authorship or editing, see Peter Groves, 'Better than it sounds: originality of musical works' [2005] Ent LR 20.

Artistic works

Copyright subsists in an artistic work irrespective of artistic quality. It will cover purely utilitarian or functional works as well as 'works of art'. This is not the case with works of artistic craftsmanship, where more than originality and fixation is needed for copyright to arise.

KEY STATUTE

Section 4(1) and (2) Copyright, Designs and Patents Act 1988

An artistic work means a graphic work (painting, drawing, diagram, map, chart or plan), a photograph, sculpture (which includes a cast or model made for the purposes of sculpture), collage, all irrespective of artistic quality. It also includes a work of architecture (a building; a fixed structure or a model for a building) or a work of artistic craftsmanship.

We can see that the meaning of 'sculpture' is very wide but it must be a three-dimensional work. The wooden models used as a mould to make the Frisbee were held to be sculptures. Although there have been attempts to demand that a hand of a sculptor must be involved in the creation of a sculpture, purely functional items are still protected. The scallop-shaped moulds of a toasted sandwich maker were held to be a sculpture even though no artist was involved in their creation, but the mere placing of random articles in a swimming pool was not.

Artistic craftsmanship

Many items could be regarded as works of craftsmanship, such as jewellery or hand-knitted jumpers. By including the word 'artistic' in s 4(1) some artistic quality is obviously required in order to gain copyright protection.

Problem area: Overlap with design right

Artistic works, especially artistic craftsmanship, present a category that causes special problems because it overlaps with design law, and the relationship between copyright and design law is not at all clear-cut.

KEY CASE

George Hensher Ltd v Restawhile Upholstery Ltd [1974] AC 64, HL

Concerning: What is needed to be a work of artistic craftsmanship

Facts

The claimant made a rough prototype for a suite of furniture in order to show how it was going to look when produced. The defendant copied the prototype and was unsuccessfully sued for copyright infringement as the work did not fit into the category of artistic craftsmanship.

Legal principle

There was no one legal principle to determine artistic craftsmanship, but solutions offered by the court were

(1) It must give pleasure and be valued for its appearance.
(2) It is up to the court to decide after talking to expert witnesses.
(3) The author must be consciously trying to create a work of art.
(4) There must be genuine craftsmanship involved.

It seems that the designer must be trying to make the product have some artistic or at least aesthetic appeal. Alternatively, it must give pleasure to others, possibly due to its skilled craftsmanship. Such an intention of course could not have existed when making a rough mock-up. We are left with a considerable amount of uncertainty in this area.

■ Secondary or derivative works

Sound recordings, films and broadcasts

Derivative works are usually, but do not have to be, based on original works which may have their own separate copyright. Derivative works typically protect the entrepreneur rather than the author of a work. It is the entrepreneur who will take any infringement proceedings if the work is copied. There is no requirement that these works be original but they must be recorded. The definition of recording is broad, to allow for the development of new technologies.

Sound recordings

KEY STATUTE

Section 5A Copyright, Designs and Patents Act 1988

(1)(a) 'Sound recordings must be a recording of sounds from which sounds may be reproduced'

A sound recording of for example birdsong, not a 'work' as defined under the Act, would also gain protection. There is no quality requirement.

Films

KEY STATUTE

Section 5B Copyright, Designs and Patents Act 1988

Film means a recording on any medium from which a moving image may be produced. The sound track accompanying a film is part of the film.

As well as the 'medium', the video tape or celluloid, being protected, a film is also protected as a dramatic work (*Norowzian* v *Arks*). The soundtrack of a film is regarded as part of the film. There is however copyright only in the master copy of the film or sound recording. This prevents a potential everlasting copyright which would otherwise result if a new copyright arose every time a CD or video tape is reproduced.

Broadcasts

KEY STATUTE

Section 6 Copyright, Designs and Patents Act 1988

Broadcast means an electronic transmission of visual images, sound or other information which is transmitted either for simultaneous reception by members of the public and capable of being lawfully received by them, or transmitted at a time determined solely by the person making the transmission for presentation to members of the public.

Most forms of internet transmission are not regarded as broadcasts, being excluded by section 6(1A). However, conventional radio or television broadcasts are included. No fixation is required. Satellite broadcasts by their very nature can reach other countries. They may there be rebroadcast to further countries before being finally broadcast to the public. They are regarded as broadcasts even if they are encrypted, as long as the public has had the decoding equipment lawfully made available to them. The law governing the broadcast is to be that of the country from where the original broadcast was made, the up-leg.

Typographical arrangements of published editions

A book may be of an original work but the typographical arrangement, the layout, font and lettering of the page, will attract its own separate copyright. This copyright will exist even if the original work is out of copyright unless it is a mere copy of a previous text. The whole book, dramatic or musical work is protected. This means the entire 'between the covers' work. So taking an article from a newspaper is not an infringement of the typographical arrangement as it is not sufficiently substantial.

■ Qualification

Works have to pass one more hurdle in order to gain copyright protection in the UK. Not only must the work be original and in tangible form but it must also be a qualifying work. Due to the Berne Convention, the Universal Copyright Convention and the TRIPS agreement authors connected with another Member State are to be treated in the same way as a Member State's own authors and should receive the same copyright. Either the author of the work, or the country of first publication (so the work must actually be published), or, in the case of a broadcast, the country of first transmission must have some connection with a Member State.

> **KEY STATUTE**
>
> **Sections 154 and 155 Copyright, Designs and Patents Act 1988**
>
> A work will qualify for copyright protection either if the author is a British citizen, domiciled or resident in the UK or a body incorporated under the law of the UK or a qualifying country or if the work was first published or published simultaneously in a qualifying country.

Either the author has a connection with a qualifying country or the work was first published in a qualifying country. Even if the work is first published in a non-qualifying country it will be regarded as first published for qualification purposes if it was then published in a qualifying country within 30 days of that initial publication. To amount to publication sufficient copies must be issued to the public to satisfy reasonable demands. So if the public shows little demand for the work few copies need be made available to qualify for publication status.

▌Duration of copyright

The duration of copyright in most of the 'original works' and in films is life of the author plus 70 years, at least 50 years for sound recordings, 50 years for broadcasts and 25 years for typographical arrangements of published editions. The duration of copyright in certain types of artistic works that have been commercially exploited is also 25 years.

Chapter summary:
Putting it all together

☐ Can you tick all the points from the revision checklist at the beginning of this chapter?

☐ Take the **end-of-chapter quiz** on the companion website.

☐ Test your knowledge of the cases below with the **revision flashcards** on the website.

☐ Attempt the essay question from the beginning of the chapter using the guidelines below.

☐ Go to the companion website to try out other questions.

Answer guidelines

See the essay question at the start of the chapter.

Points to remember when answering this question

■ Some of the further reading below would be helpful in answering this question.

■ The key case which indicated that TV show formats were not adequately protected by copyright was the Privy Council decision in *Green* v *Broadcasting Corp of New Zealand* [1989] RPC 700, the 'Opportunity Knocks' case. This is a useful starting point for the discussion.

■ Identify in that case why the format was not protected. For example, written scripts had not been produced in evidence and the format as claimed was described as being too uncertain.

■ Consider and discuss other cases such as *Norowzian* v *Arks (No 2)* [2000] FSR 363, the 'jump-cutting' film.

■ Note that lack of protection means that countries such as the US, Australia and New Zealand can copy formats of UK TV shows. For example, New Zealand makes *Popstars* which is very similar to *Pop Idol*.

■ It would be useful to consider cases on non-literal copying, such as *Nova Productions Ltd* v *Mazooma Games Ltd* [2007] RPC 25 and *IPC Media Ltd* v *Highbury Leisure Publishing (No 2)* [2005] FSR 20, where what was being claimed in reality was that the format of the video game and glossy magazine had been copied.

Make your answer stand out

■ Consider what, if anything, producers of TV shows could do to acquire some protection through copyright law.

■ Set out your views on whether copyright should be extended to include formats as a distinct type of copyright and the implications this might have, for example, by making it difficult to bring out rival 'copycat' shows.

FURTHER READING

Gravells, N. 'Authorship and originality: the persistent influence of Walter v Lane' [2007] IPQ 267.

Klement, U. 'Protecting television show formats under copyright law – new developments in common law and civil law countries' [2007] 2 EIPR 52.

Steffensen, T. 'Rights to TV Formats – from a copyright and marketing law perspective' [2000] Ent LR 85.

2
Authorship, ownership and moral rights

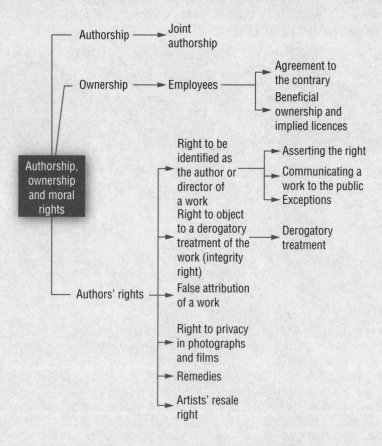

A printable version of this topic map is available from www.pearsoned.co.uk/lawexpress

Revision checklist

Essential points you should know:

- [ ] Authorship and joint authorship.
- [ ] Author or employer as first owner.
- [ ] The paternity right.
- [ ] The integrity right.
- [ ] False attribution of a work.
- [ ] Right to privacy in photographs and films.

Introduction

The identity of an author will determine first ownership and consequently the duration of both the copyright and moral rights in the work.

In order to exploit copyright you must have the right to do so by ownership or licence. The author, the person who creates the work, is normally the first owner of the copyright. However, if the work was created in the course of employment, the employer will usually be the first owner of the copyright. Two independent rights exist: moral rights, which may be retained by the author even though ownership has been assigned, and an economic right, the right to exploit the work. The owner or author may exploit the work himself or may license (retaining ownership), or assign (transferring ownership), the copyright to another.

Assessment advice

Essay questions

An essay question may well ask you to consider the weakness of the moral rights that have been given to authors in the UK. The vulnerable bargaining position of the author and the fact that many of these rights can be waived is of significance. You must keep in mind when answering such a question that very strong rights for authors reduce the efficiency with which the entrepreneur can exploit the work that has been assigned to him. Strengthening the moral rights may have an impact on the willingness of the entrepreneur to commercialise the author's work in the long term.

Assessment advice

Problem questions

Many copyright works are created by employees during the course of their employment. It is highly likely that there will be some issue relating to the rights of first ownership in any problem question set in this area. Problems around unintentional joint authorship may also be included and you must be able to establish clearly the elements that are needed to be regarded as a joint author rather than a mere provider of ideas.

Sample question

Could you answer this question? Below is a typical problem question that could arise on this topic. Guidelines on answering the question are included at the end of this chapter, whilst a sample essay question and guidance on tackling it can be found on the companion website.

PROBLEM QUESTION

Adrian wrote the music and lyrics for a song called 'Bad'. Having trouble with the drum beat he heard Betty, a carpenter, hammering in the house next door. Inviting Betty into his studio he asked her to hammer while he played the tune in time to her rhythm. He recorded the resulting music. Adrian sold the song to BMI but is upset that they have made his 'Grime' music into a ballad. He feels that his reputation as a 'Grime' musician has been destroyed. Adrian has discovered that Chris has produced a CD in which he is falsely said to be the author of the song 'Nasty'. Betty has seen that one of her wedding photographs taken by 'Happy Day Photos' is featured on the cover of Chris's CD.
Discuss.

■ Authorship

The author of an original work is the person who created it. The author of a compilation is the person who gathers or organises the material contained within the compilation, while each separate contribution will have its own separate author.

KEY STATUTE

Section 9(1) Copyright, Designs and Patents Act 1988

The author is the person who created the work. Depending on the type of work, this includes the producer, the director, the person making a broadcast, the publisher or the person who made the arrangements necessary for the creation of the work. A work will be held to be of unknown authorship if it is not possible to identify the author after making reasonable enquiries.

The author is the person who puts in the right sort of effort, skill and labour into the creation or expression of the work. There must be that essential creative input, a 'direct responsibility for what actually appears on the paper'. An amanuensis or secretary taking dictation, although responsible for fixation, is not the author of the work.

REVISION NOTE

Please refer to Chapter 1 for discussion on fixation and the case of *Walter* v Lane.

It is easier to determine the author of an original work than the author of a derivative work. On the whole, the author of a derivative work is the person who makes the necessary arrangements for the making of the work. This would be the producer of a sound recording or the producer and principle director of a film, the person making a broadcast and the publisher of the typographical arrangement of a published edition.

Joint authorship

If people have collaborated so that it is impossible to identify each author's contribution, this will result in a work of joint authorship.

KEY STATUTE

Section 10(1) Copyright, Designs and Patents Act 1988

A work is of joint authorship if produced by the collaboration of two or more authors and the contribution of each is not distinct from that of the others.

The authors need not have intended to create a work of joint authorship and their contributions need not be equal. But they must have intended to create a work.

KEY CASE

Hodgens v *Beckingham* [2003] EMLR 376, CA

Concerning: a claim to joint authorship

Facts

Mr Hodgens wrote a song, 'Young at Heart', for the band Bananarama. While recording the song in the studio Mr Hodgens asked Mr Valentino, a session musician, to add some 'jiggy' violin solo parts demonstrating the chord structure he wanted to be used. Mr Valentino successfully claimed to be joint author of the song as his contribution was significant and original.

KEY CASE

Legal principle

There is no need to prove an intention on the part of the authors to create a joint work. The principal test is that parties are engaged in a joint labouring in the furtherance of a common design.

EXAM TIP

Show that you understand the practical significance of this decision. This case demonstrates how important it is to make sure that there has been an assignment of copyright from not only session musicians but anyone else who may have a creative input into an author's work.

To be a joint author each must have made a significant contribution in terms of the right sort of creative skill and judgment. Merely editing, contributing suggestions, ideas and information will not give rise to a finding of joint authorship.

KEY CASE

Robin Ray v *Classic FM plc* [1998] FSR 622 ChD

Concerning: The type of contribution needed to become a joint author

Facts

Robin Ray was an expert on classical music and after discussion of what was needed created a play list of music for the use of the radio station Classic FM. Classic FM failed in their claim that they were joint authors of the list having provided the ideas. Copyright does not exist in ideas but the expression of the ideas, and Ray had not only written down but was solely responsible for the ideas found in the play list.

Legal principle

To be a joint author there must be a significant creative contribution which was incorporated into the finished work.

'Although penmanship did not have to be exercised, a joint author had to have direct responsibility for what ended up on the paper which was the equivalent to penmanship' (Mr. Justice Lightman).

Each of the joint authors will have their own copyright in the work, which if an original work will last for the life of the longest to live plus 70 years. Although a joint author can leave their share on death, consent of all the co-authors must be obtained in order to license the work.

KEY DEFINITION

Joint/co-authorship: A work of joint authorship is where the contribution of each author cannot be separated, whereas the contribution of each author in a work of co-authorship is distinct, discrete and separately distinguishable.

Ownership

Subject to some exceptions, the author of a work is the first owner of the copyright.

KEY STATUTE

Section 11(1) and (2) Copyright, Designs and Patents Act 1988

The author of a work is the first owner of any copyright in it. However, if made by an employee in the course of their employment, the employer is the first owner of any copyright subject to any agreement to the contrary.

The main difficulty with the ownership provisions concerns the employer/employee relationship and the meaning of 'in the course of his employment'.

Employees

The job description in the contract of employment is important. A person employed in a factory who writes poetry in their spare time is not employed as a poet and the poems are not written in the course of their employment. They, not their employer, will be the first owner of the copyright in the poems. However, if the employee is employed under a contract with a very wide job description as a researcher, copyright in a research proposal will probably belong to the employer, even if the employee created the work on his own initiative outside normal working hours.

KEY CASE

Stephenson Jordan & Harrison Ltd v *MacDonald* [1952] RPC 10, CA

Concerning: Whether copyright belonged to an employee or employer

Facts

An accountant started to give lectures. He published them in a book. Although his employer had provided secretarial help when he was writing the book, he nevertheless owned the copyright in the book. He was employed to advise clients. Giving lectures was not part of his normal duties and he had not been instructed by his employers either to give the lectures or produce the book. The copyrights in a report written for a client as part of the employee's duties and incorporated into a part of the book did however belong to the employer.

Legal principle

Merely using the facilities of an employer does not entitle them to copyright in an employee's creation if it was not made in the course of their duties as an employee.

You should ask whether the skill, effort and judgment expended by the employee in creating the work are part of the employee's normal duties (express or implied) or within any special duties assigned to him by the employer. If they are not, the employee will be the first owner of the copyright, even if he has used his employer's facilities when creating the work.

Agreement to the contrary

If there is an agreement to the contrary, either express or implied, the employee may remain the first owner of the copyright.

EXAM TIP

Normally in a transfer of ownership an assignment will not be effective unless it is in writing and signed. However, no writing is needed where an employer as first owner agrees to an employee's being first owner.

The agreement to the contrary would usually be between the employer and the employee but if the employee has done work on behalf of a third party it may be between the employer and the third party. If the employee's name appears on the work, or copies of the work, there is a presumption that the work was not made in the course of employment.

Beneficial ownership and implied licences

If a consultant has been commissioned to create a work they are *not* an employee and the commissioner, unlike an employer, has no right to the copyright in the work. The commissioner may not realise that to obtain copyright in the work a written assignment would need to have been made. In some circumstances the court may decide that it is equitable to hold that the commissioner is entitled to beneficial ownership of the copyright or that a licence should be implied.

Blair v *Osborne & Tomkins* [1971] 1 All ER 468, CA

Concerning: An implied licence to use a commissioned work

Facts

The owner of land commissioned architects to make plans in order to obtain planning permission to build houses. The owners then sold the land. The purchasers asked surveyors to modify the plans and then used them to build the houses.

Legal principle

Although architects own the copyright in their plans there may be a licence implied to allow the work to be used for its intended purpose.

■ Authors' rights

UK copyright law has traditionally emphasised the economic rights associated with copyright. Efficient exploitation of the work requires as much freedom for the entrepreneur as possible. However, this emphasis on the rights of the entrepreneur created an imbalance and this has been in part rectified by the introduction of the moral rights. They give authors some stake in their work after they have assigned ownership and no longer have control over how it is used. These moral rights are the right to be acknowledged as the author, the right to object to modification and derogatory treatment of the work, a right not to have another's work falsely attributed to them and a right to privacy in certain photographs and films. There is in addition the *droit de suite*, which gives authors of works of art and manuscripts a royalty when the work is resold.

Although on the face of it these rights seem to be of great benefit to the authors of works they lose much of their force as they can be waived. Many authors are not capable of exploiting their own works and must assign them. They may be under great pressure from the entrepreneur to waive these moral rights to allow unfettered use of the work. In addition, some rights may fail for lack of positive assertion on the part of the author or director.

Right to be identified as the author or director of a work

Also referred to as the 'paternity right', this is the right of the person who brought the work to life.

Sections 77–79 Copyright, Designs and Patents Act 1988

The author of an original work and director of a film have the right to be identified as the author or director of the work. The right arises when the work or an adaptation of the work is published commercially, performed in public, or copies of a film, sound recording or graphic work representing a work of architecture are issued to or communicated to the public.

The right must be asserted either at the time of the assignment or licensing of the copyright or in writing signed by the author.

There are exceptions to the right which include computer-related works, works created during the course of employment, fair dealing exceptions or where it would be impractical to include the author's name with the publication.

Problem area

There is an inconsistency in the treatment of the lyrics for songs in the Act. Unlike the economic rights, a literary work for the purposes of the moral rights does not include words intended to be sung or spoken with music.

Asserting the right

The right to be identified as the author of an 'original' work or as the director of a film does not arise automatically, it must be asserted. The right applies in relation to the whole or any substantial part of the work which is in copyright. Substantial in the context of moral rights will have the same meaning as applies for economic rights.

REVISION NOTE

See Chapter 3 for a discussion on the meaning of 'substantial'.

The identification must be clear and reasonably prominent. An artist putting their name or a pseudonym on a painting is asserting their right. Although the paternity right may be asserted at any time during the life of the author, this assertion will only bind those with notice of it.

EXAM TIP

Because there is a stronger right if asserted at the time of assignment of the copyright, you should point out that it is therefore wise to include a document asserting moral rights at the same time as the transfer of the economic rights. Then it will not only bind the assignee, but also anyone to whom the assignee assigns part of his rights, even without notice of the assertion.

Once asserted, the right to be identified as the author springs into action. However, the right only relates to the commercialisation of the work and does not apply to derivative works.

Communicating a work to the public

Communicating a work to the public means communication via any means including broadcasting. Non-commercial exploitation, such as the private performance of a play, does not give rise to the obligation to identify the author. But once asserted, *every* commercial publication must be accompanied by the name of the author of the initial work.

Exceptions

There is a long list of exceptions to the paternity right. They include computer software, computer-generated works, newspapers, encyclopaedias and an exception relating to disc jockeys and employees in the course of their employment. It is felt that without these exemptions the exploitation of the work could be hampered by so many people asserting their moral rights. There are also fair dealing exceptions where the right to name the author will not be enforced.

Right to object to derogatory treatment of the work (integrity right)

> **KEY STATUTE**
>
> **Sections 80–83 Copyright, Designs and Patents Act 1988**
>
> The author of an original work and directors of a film have the right not to have their work subjected to derogatory treatment. Treatment means the addition to, deletion from, alteration to or adaptation of the work but does not include translation, arrangement or transcription which is merely a change of key or register of a musical work. Treatment is derogatory if it amounts to distortion or mutilation of the work or is prejudicial to the honour or reputation of the author or director.
>
> The right only applies if the derogatory treatment of the original work is published commercially or is issued to the public.
>
> There are exceptions for computer-related works and works created for the purpose of reporting current events, where it would be impractical to apply the right.
>
> The right only applies if the author has been identified and if no disclaimer has been included.

The 'integrity right' applies to works that are in copyright and benefits the same people as the paternity right but need not be asserted.

Derogatory treatment

Derogatory treatment is a treatment which amounts to distortion or mutilation of the work. The work itself must be altered. It is not enough that the work is displayed in a way that would be regarded as derogatory. However, distortion or mutilation of the work itself is not enough. There must also be prejudice to the honour or reputation of the author.

KEY CASE

Confetti Records v *Warner Music UK Ltd* [2003] EWHC 1724 (ChD)

Concerning: Derogatory treatment

Facts

A Rap version of the song 'Burnin'', was made by the group Heartless Crew. The Rap version contained references to violence and drugs which the court found very difficult to decipher. The original composer Mr Alcee unsuccessfully claimed that the addition of the Rap lyrics was a derogatory treatment of his work.

Legal principle

There must be some damage to the author's honour or reputation.
'I hold that the mere fact that a work has been distorted or mutilated gives rise to no claim, unless the distortion or mutilation prejudices the author's honour or reputation.' (Mr Justice Lewison)

It is not up to the author but to the right-thinking member of the public to decide if the reputation of the author has been prejudiced by the derogatory treatment. As with the paternity right there are exceptions, and the right does not apply to computer programs and computer-generated works or in relation to any work made for the purpose of reporting current events, newspapers, magazines, encyclopaedias, or to employees. It is felt that being able to object to such treatment in these areas would cause potential delay in publishing these works.

False attribution of a work

This right is again concerned with commercial not private communications.

KEY STATUTE

Section 84 Copyright, Designs and Patents Act 1988

The author of an original work and directors of a film have the right not to have a work either expressly or impliedly falsely attributed to them. The right applies if the falsely attributed work is issued to the public by a person who knows or has reason to believe that the attribution is false.

The right also applies if in the course of a business a person knowingly possesses or deals with the work or a copy of the work which contains the false attribution.

The false attribution right applies to original works and films, as do the other moral rights. There are no exceptions so it is also relevant to computer programs and typefaces. It can be used where B writes a book and pretends it, or parts of it, were written by A. False attribution does not relate to a work created by the person asserting it. As A, the person falsely attributed, has no copyright in the work its duration is not the life of the author plus 70 years but only 20 years after the death of A, the person to whom the work is attributed falsely. There is also a right of action against anyone who possesses or deals with a copy of the work in the course of business if they know or have reason to believe that there is a false attribution.

Right to privacy in photographs and films

There is no general right to privacy in English law. When someone commissions a photograph it is the photographer who is the first owner of the copyright in the photograph. The photographer has control over the negatives and can use them for his or her own purposes even against the wishes of the commissioner.

KEY STATUTE

Section 85 Copyright, Designs and Patents Act 1988

A person who commissions the taking of a photograph or the making of a film for private and domestic purpose has the right not to have copies of the work issued, exhibited, shown or communicated to the public.

The right to privacy applies in the case of a photograph or film which is in copyright. The photograph must have been taken only for private and domestic purposes. It must have been commissioned. The right will not apply if a photographer took a photograph entirely on his own initiative or the subject of the photograph was included incidentally. The photographer does not need to be a professional photographer and the term is for the work itself, life of the author, the photographer, plus 70 years.

Remedies

Injunctions and damages are normally available for a breach of a statutory duty. If there has been an infringement of moral rights, damages would be for non-economic loss because moral rights are not economic in nature. An appropriate remedy may however be requiring a disclaimer dissociating the author or director from any derogatory treatment of their work.

Artists' resale right

This right was brought in under the Artists Resale Right Regulations 2006/346. It applies to original works of graphic or plastic art such as paintings and sculptures that are still in copyright. It does not apply if the work is sold privately. The author is given a right which they may not transfer or waive but may be transmitted on death. The author of the work is entitled to receive a royalty payable by the seller which is a percentage of the resale price, up to a maximum which is at present 10,000 Euro.

Chapter summary:
Putting it all together

Answer guidelines

See the problem question at the start of the chapter.

Points to remember when answering this question
This problem concerns the ownership and moral rights of authors of original works.

- Adrian is the author and therefore first owner of the copyright in the song 'Bad' (s9).
- If it is impossible to identify each author's contribution (s10) and Betty had contributed the right sort of skill and labour into creating the beat and if the intention had been to create a 'work' she could be a joint owner of the song (*Hodgens* v *Beckingham*). Merely contributing ideas would not be sufficient; she must be responsible for what was actually recorded (*Ray* v *Classic FM*).
- Adrian could claim that his integrity right will be infringed if the altered work is issued to the public (ss 80–83). He must prove that there has been some derogatory treatment to the work itself. It is not up to him but up to the right-thinking member of the public to feel that his reputation has been prejudiced by the derogatory treatment (*Confetti Records*). Here it is unlikely that such a person would feel that such alteration would be sufficiently derogatory to his reputation.
- Adrian can also complain that Chris has made a false attribution by falsely claiming he is the author of 'Nasty'. This right will last for 20 years after Adrian's death.
- Betty has a right to privacy in her wedding photos as long as she commissioned 'Happy Day Photos' to take them and they were intended purely for domestic purposes, unlike *Douglas* v *Hello!*

Make your answer stand out

■ Point out that Adrian should have asked Betty to assign her rights to him.

■ Also mention that Chris's record company will be dealing with copies and so they can also be sued.

■ Explain that although Betty may be able to take advantage of the privacy right if there had been an intention to use the photographs commercially, as in *Douglas* v *Hello*, this right would not be available.

FURTHER READING

Calleja, R. 'Copyright: equitable owners of copyright in Dr Martens–AirWair logo' [2005] 5 Ent LR N44.

Chan, P. 'Moral rights in university students' academic works' [2007] 3 JIPLP 174.

Longdin, L. 'Collaborative authorship of distance learning materials: cross-border copyright and moral rights problems' [2005] 1 EIPR 4.

3
Copyright infringement, defences and remedies

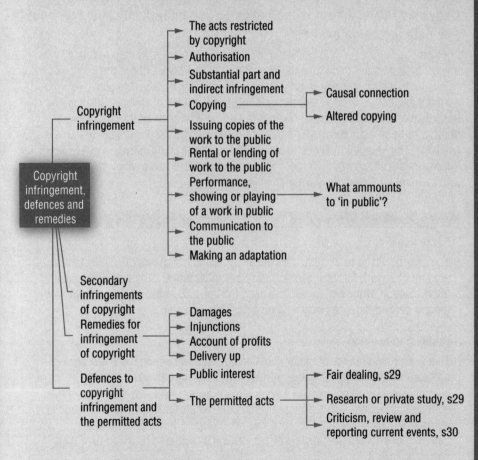

A printable version of this topic map is available from www.pearsoned.co.uk/lawexpress

Revision checklist

Essential points you should know:

- [ ] The acts restricted by copyright.
- [ ] What amounts to copying and the communication to the public.
- [ ] Secondary infringements of copyright.
- [ ] Remedies for infringement of copyright.
- [ ] Defences to copyright infringement and the permitted acts.

◼ Introduction

Copyright infringement is the making of unauthorised copies without any defence being available.

The owner of copyright is given exclusive rights in respect of certain restricted acts. If any of these acts are done to a substantial part of the work without the licence of the owner there will be primary infringement. There are other restricted activities, of a commercial nature, such as dealing with infringing copies of a work. These are described as secondary infringement. It is also an infringement if you authorise another to do a restricted act. There are not only civil but also criminal remedies available. The criminal offences generally, though not exactly, mirror the secondary infringements of copyright. There are exceptions or defences to copyright infringement known as the permitted acts.

Assessment advice

Essay questions

You may be asked to discuss the difficulty in establishing what is a substantial amount of a work for infringement purposes. Alternatively, the balance needed in the protection of the author and the need for freedom of expression in relation to the fair dealing defences may also be a possible question.

Problem questions

This is a prime area for problem questions. A scenario where there has been some conscious or unconscious infringement, possibly an adaptation or alternatively altered copying, of a work is very likely. There may also be some commercial dealing with the work by someone who claims they do not have the necessary knowledge that the work was an infringing work. There may be defences of criticism and review or fair dealing available to the defendant that you must identify.

Sample question

Could you answer this question? Below is a typical essay question that could arise on this topic. Guidelines on answering the question are included at the end of this chapter, whilst a sample problem question and guidance on tackling it can be found on the companion website.

In *Designers Guild Ltd* v *Russell Williams (Textiles) Ltd* [2001] FSR 113, Lord Hoffmann said at para 26:

'Generally speaking, in cases of artistic copyright, the more abstract and simple the copied idea, the less likely it is to constitute a substantial part. Originality, in the sense of the contribution of the author's skill and labour, tends to lie in the detail with which the basic idea is presented. Copyright law protects foxes better than hedgehogs.'

Discuss this statement in relation to what constitutes a substantial part of a work for the purposes of infringement.

■ Copyright infringement

The acts restricted by copyright

Copyright is the exclusive right given to the owner to copy the work, or do any of the restricted acts in relation to the work.

KEY STATUTE

Section 16(1) and (2) Copyright, Designs and Patents Act 1988

The owner of the copyright in a work has the exclusive right to copy; issue copies of the work, rent, lend, perform, show, play or communicate the work to the public. They have the right to make an adaptation of the work or do any of the above in relation to an adaptation.

Copyright in a work is infringed by a person who without the licence of the copyright owner does, or authorises another to do, any of the acts restricted by copyright.

The owner may grant a licence to another to do any of these restricted acts.

Authorisation

Not only is it an infringement to perform one of the restricted acts but also to authorise another to do so. In other jurisdictions libraries have been held to have authorised copyright infringement by providing photocopiers without any warnings to the users or supervision against copyright infringement. However, in the UK merely making copying equipment available will only amount to authorisation if there has actually been some encouragement or at least turning a blind eye to infringement.

Authorise. To 'authorise' means to grant or purport to grant to a third person the right to do the act complained of.

KEY CASE

CBS Songs Ltd v *Amstrad Consumer Electronics plc* [1988] 1 AC 1013, HL

Concerning: Whether providing machines which could be used for copyright infringement was authorising infringement

Facts

Amstrad was held not to be authorising copyright infringement by the sale of its twin deck tape recorder machines which could be used to copy music, therefore infringing its copyright.

Legal principle

Merely facilitating unauthorised copying was not authorisation if the machines could be used for legitimate purposes.

Amstrad had not authorised the infringement even though their machines may have facilitated it. They had conferred a power but not a right to copy. This question is relevant to file-to-file sharing and the question should be, can the equipment be used for legitimate purposes and has the manufacturer/internet service provider got control?

Substantial part and indirect infringement

If an article such as a drawer is made according to a drawing, unauthorised copies of the drawer will indirectly infringe the copyright subsisting in the drawing. Not only copying the whole, but also copying a substantial amount of the work, will amount to infringement.

Section 16(3)(a) and (b) Copyright, Designs and Patents Act 1988

The copying must be in relation to the work as a whole or any substantial part of it and can occur either directly or indirectly.

It can be difficult to determine what a substantial amount is. There are no guidelines in the Act and different types of work are treated differently. Substantial must be decided by the quality of what has been taken rather than the quantity. If what has been copied is commonplace, an idea or fact, it will not normally be regarded as original enough to amount to a substantial part. However, taking part of a compilation of unoriginal material may be a substantial exercise of skill or judgment of the person creating the compilation. A small portion of a work, if the most memorable or valuable part such as the hook in a piece of music, can be substantial.

Problem area: Approach to determining substantial amount

Identify the parts taken by the defendant, then isolate them from the remainder of the defendant's work and only then consider whether those parts represent a substantial part of the claimant's work.

Assume I reproduce the smile of the Mona Lisa (pretend it is still in copyright). I use the smile as a small portion of my work. To decide if I have taken a substantial part of Leonardo Da Vinci's work, look at how memorable a part the smile is and how important it is to Da Vinci's work, not how important it is to mine. Keep in mind that if the defendant is competing with the claimant, this would be taken into account.

EXAM TIP

Point out that if the courts concentrate on quality to determine substantiality they may end up demanding merit of the copyright work, and for original works no merit is required.

The importance of the work cannot be the test for all works. With computer programs a very minor piece of punctuation that took little skill or judgment to create may be important, in that the software will not work without it. It does not mean that copying that full stop is taking a substantial part of the whole program.

REVISION NOTE

For a discussion of the quality requirements of copyright works please refer to Chapter 1.

If there has been regular cumulative copying of trivial amounts of a work, this cannot amount to a substantial part. Whether what has been taken is trivial may depend on how you look at the work itself. Small extracts taken from magazine articles where the typographical arrangement has been copied would be regarded as trivial if the 'work' is regarded as the whole magazine rather than each individual article within the magazine.

Copying

What amounts to copying varies depending on the nature of the work in question.

KEY STATUTE

Section 17 Copyright, Designs and Patents Act 1988

Copying, in relation to a literary, dramatic, musical or artistic work, means reproducing the work in any material form including storing the work in any medium by electronic means. Copying an artistic work includes making a copy of a two-dimensional work in three dimensions and vice versa, or making a photograph of the whole or any substantial part of a film or broadcast. Copying of all types of work includes the making of copies which are transient or incidental to some other use of the work.

Consequently, unauthorised recording of any works of copyright by any method, even if transient or incidental, will infringe. Taking a single photograph of a substantial part of one frame of a film or an internet webpage infringes copyright. However, 'dimensional shift' or making a three-dimensional work out of a two-dimensional work applies only to artistic works. If a knitting pattern – a literary work – is made into a jumper – a three-dimensional object – there will be no copying. Infringement will however occur if there is 'reverse engineering' such as where a car exhaust is made from a drawing and also where actors in three dimensions enact a two-dimensional cartoon.

Causal connection

If two people each independently take a photograph of Buckingham Palace, even though the photographs may look identical there is no copying. To show infringement the claimant must first prove that the defendant has copied either consciously or unconsciously. They must show prior access to the copyright work. Once a case is made out, the burden of proof shifts to the defendant, who must then give an explanation of why there are similarities between the works.

Altered copying

If the defendant has copied the whole of a work there is little problem apart from proof. If there have been considerable alterations it is more difficult to prove. The court has to decide whether the defendant's work incorporates a substantial part of the skill and labour involved in the creation of the claimant's work.

KEY CASE

Designers Guild Ltd v *Russell Williams Ltd* [2001] FSR 113, HL

Concerning: Altered copying

Facts

The claimant successfully sued for infringement of the copyright in an impressionistic fabric design comprising stripes with flowers scattered around the design. The defendant created a design based on a similar idea of stripes and scattered flowers. It looked very similar but there were many differences.

Legal principle

The test is whether the infringer had incorporated a substantial amount of the independent skill and labour of the author. You must look at the claimant's work and the importance and the amount of the work taken from that, not the importance of it to the work of the defendant. The cumulative effect of those similarities ought to be considered, but ideas or commonplace things will not be included.

FURTHER THINKING

Ronan Deazley, 'Copyright in the House of Lords: recent cases, juridical reasoning and academic writing' [2004] IPQ 121.

The author considers two House of Lords cases on substantial part. Discusses the idea/expression debate and whether the balance is becoming weighed too much in favour of the author with the potential that creativity will be inhibited.

Issuing copies of the work to the public

This concerns exhaustion of rights and the free movement of goods within the European Economic Area (EEA). It applies to all categories of works.

> **KEY STATUTE**
>
> **Section 18 Copyright, Designs and Patents Act 1988**
>
> Issuing copies of the work to the public includes putting them into circulation in the EEA when copies have not previously been put into circulation there either by or with the consent of the copyright owner, or outside the EEA when copies have not previously been put into circulation in the EEA or elsewhere.
>
> Issuing to the public does not include subsequent distribution, sale, hiring or loan of copies previously put into circulation or subsequent importation of such copies into the UK or another EEA state.

Consequently, the copyright owner can take action against anyone who for the first time issues a copy of his work to the public anywhere without his consent. He loses control over any copies once he puts them into circulation in the EEA. If he first issued the copy in France or another EEA country but not the UK, he cannot prevent someone importing a copy from France into the UK and selling it. If he first issues the copy in the USA he can prevent its importation into the EEA. It should be noted that this right to issue applies to each and every copy of the work.

Rental or lending of work to the public

The right applies to the 'original' works of copyright films and sound recordings. The rental or lending of the DVDs or CDs (unless done privately) after the owner has issued them to the public gives rise to a right to obtain a royalty.

> **KEY STATUTE**
>
> **Section 18A Copyright, Designs and Patents Act 1988**
>
> Rental is making a copy of the work available for use, on terms that it will or may be returned, for direct or indirect economic or commercial advantage.
>
> Lending is making a copy of the work available for use, on terms that it will or may be returned, otherwise than for direct or indirect economic or commercial advantage, through an establishment which is accessible to the public.

Where an author of an original work agrees to its inclusion in a film, it is assumed that the author has assigned his rental rights in relation to that film and instead acquires a right to an equitable remuneration.

Performance, showing or playing of a work in public

In a literary, dramatic or musical work, but not an artistic work, these are restricted acts.

> **KEY STATUTE**
>
> **Section 19(2) and (3) Copyright, Designs and Patents Act 1988**
>
> A performance includes the delivery of lectures, addresses, speeches and sermons and includes any mode of visual or acoustic presentation, including presentation by means of a sound recording, film or broadcast.
>
> The playing or showing of the work in public is an act restricted by the copyright in a sound recording, film or broadcast.

The person in charge of the equipment used in playing music to members of the public, for example background music in a café, is the one infringing. A 'blanket' licence to allow such use may be obtained from the Performing Right Society.

What amounts to 'in public'?

A performance will be regarded as a public performance unless the audience is of a domestic nature. If payment is made there is no doubt that this will involve performance in public. There can be grey areas such as when a hotel provides music to the guests in their private rooms. The main question should be whether the performance of the work conflicts with the copyright owner's right to be paid a royalty.

Communication to the public

This is a restricted act in relation to the original works, a sound recording, film or broadcast.

> **KEY STATUTE**
>
> **Section 20 Copyright, Designs and Patents Act 1988**
>
> Communication to the public means communication or making available to the public an original work or broadcast by electronic transmission so that the public can access it from a place and at a time individually chosen by them.

Placing a work on a website or providing a hypertext link to it will infringe if the work can be downloaded by any member of the public in the UK. It does not matter where the computer on which the website is hosted is physically located.

Making an adaptation

The restricted act only applies to literary, dramatic and musical works. Artistic works are not covered by the act of making an adaptation.

REVISION NOTE

When an adaptation is made the economic rights are affected but moral rights of the author may also be infringed. Please refer to Chapter 2 on this issue.

KEY STATUTE

Section 21(3) Copyright, Designs and Patents Act 1988

Adaptation arises in relation to a literary, dramatic or musical work (other than computer programs and databases). It means a translation, a conversion of a dramatic work into a non-dramatic work or vice versa, or a version of a work in which the story or action is conveyed wholly or mainly by means of pictures into a form suitable to be reproduced in a book or periodical. In relation to a musical work it is an arrangement or transcription of the work.

REVISION NOTE

See Chapter 1 for discussion of adaptation of musical works and *Hyperion Records* v *Sawkins.*

Adaptation would include a substantial amount of a book that has been made into a play or translated, for example, from French to English. It covers an adaptation of an adaptation. If enough skill and judgment has been involved in the adaptation it may attract its own copyright, but would be infringing if done without the consent of the original owner. Adaptation does not apply to an artistic work, so an artistic work can be copied but cannot be the subject of an adaptation.

■ Secondary infringements of copyright

Secondary infringement is all about commercial 'dealing' with infringing copies. It includes providing premises for the performance of, apparatus for making or transmitting an infringing article in the course of a business. Secondary and primary infringement do not have to have been committed by the same person. For a secondary infringement the person responsible must have knowledge or reason to believe that the copies are infringing copies and that what they are doing involves a secondary infringement.

KEY STATUTE

Sections 22–26 Copyright, Designs and Patents Act 1988

Copyright is infringed by importing, possessing or 'dealing' with, selling, letting for hire, offering or exposing for sale or hire, exhibiting or distributing an infringing copy in the course of a business and in a way as to affect prejudicially the owner of the copyright. Also by permitting the use of premises or supplying the apparatus for an infringing performance knowing or having reason to believe that secondary infringement will occur.

The main issue here is the knowledge needed by the secondary infringer.

KEY CASE

LA Gear Inc v Hi-Tec Sports plc [1992] FSR 121, CA

Concerning: The meaning of 'has reason to believe' for secondary infringement

Facts

An employee of LA Gear had made a drawing for a sports shoe. It was later discovered that an identical shoe had been made by Hi-Tec Sports. Sending the defendant copies of the drawings and a letter saying they had copyright in them was held enough to make the defendant 'have reason to believe' the shoes were infringing the claimant's copyright.

Legal principle

The test must be objective: whether the reasonable man, with knowledge of the facts known to the defendant, would have formed the belief that the item was an infringing copy.

A 'reason to believe' would include a reasonable belief that the copyright had expired, did not subsist in the work, or that the copies had been made with the copyright owner's permission. Some of the criminal offences provided for under the 1988 Act closely follow the equivalent secondary infringements, and the same level of knowledge is required.

■ Remedies for infringement of copyright

The remedies applicable to civil infringement include injunctions, damages or an account of profits, delivery up and destruction orders. A maximum term of 10 years' imprisonment is available for criminal offences. If there is a very strong case to suspect copyright infringement and a likelihood of serious damage, the copyright owner (or licensee) should apply for a search order. Such an order will be granted if it is necessary to prevent the destruction of the evidence.

Damages

Damages are awarded, if not too remote, in order to compensate the copyright owner for any actual loss suffered. These may be based on a likely royalty or lost sales. Liability of the defendant is strict for the 'primary' infringements but damages will not be awarded against the defendant if they did not know, and had no reason to believe, that copyright subsisted in the work.

EXAM TIP

Point out that a wise copyright owner will apply a prominent copyright notice to copies of his work so that infringers cannot claim to be ignorant of the subsistence of copyright in the work.

Injunctions

An injunction may order a person to stop making infringing copies or to destroy something which is used for making infringing copies. Injunctions are equitable and therefore discretionary. The court must feel that there is a serious issue to be tried. Injunctions are unlikely to be granted if damages would be an adequate remedy. However, they are a very common form of protection in this area of law. Quick action often needs to be taken and it may be many years before an action would come to full trial. The court will consider on the balance of convenience the impact of granting or refusing the injunction on each of the parties.

KEY DEFINITION

Injunction. An injunction is an order of the court which prohibits an act or the commencement or continuance of an act. Alternatively, an injunction might order a person to perform some act.

Account of profits

An account of profits is intended to prevent unjust enrichment. That is the gain made by the defendant due to the infringement, not the retail value of the infringing articles. An account may be very difficult to assess. However, it may be the only monetary remedy obtainable when damages are unavailable because the defendant did not have reason to believe that copyright subsisted in the work.

Delivery up

A court may order that infringing copies, or articles designed or adapted for making copies of the copyright owner's work, are delivered up to them. The person must know or have reason to believe that the article has been or is to be used to make infringing copies. An order for the disposal of the infringing copies must also be made.

■ Defences to copyright infringement and the permitted acts

Numerous 'permitted acts' are included in the Act. There are other defences also, the most obvious being that there is no copyright in the work, that the owner had given their authority, or that less than a substantial amount of the work has been taken.

Public interest

Cases where the public interest is at issue often concern the publication of information, and frequently questions of confidence will be raised.

REVISION NOTE

Please see Chapter 4 on confidence.

The defence of public interest does not claim that there is no copyright subsisting in the work but that it is not in the public interest to enforce the right. This could be used where a work was immoral or in some way in contravention to society's values. It needs to be balanced against the right to freedom of expression which exists under the Human Rights Act.

KEY CASE

Hyde Park Residence Ltd v Yelland [2000] RPC 604, CA

Concerning: Whether the public interest defence applied to copyright infringement

Facts

The day before Diana, Princess of Wales and Dodi Al Fayed were killed in a car crash they had been recorded on video at a Paris property, with the time of their arrival and departure displayed. Stills from the video were made and published in the *Sun* newspaper to show that Mr Mohamed Al Fayed had lied about the duration of the visit. When sued for copyright infringement, the *Sun* failed in the defences of public interest and fair dealing for the purpose of reporting current events.

Legal principle

If information of interest contained within the work (the times of arrival and departure) could have been made available without infringing copyright, publication would not be necessary and the public interest defence would be unavailable.

Although the court must have regard to the right of freedom of expression, there will be no justification for copyright infringement if the necessary facts could be disclosed without such infringement.

The permitted acts

The justification for these permitted acts is that it provides a fair balance between the rights of the copyright owner and the rights of society at large. They cover such things as education, libraries and archives. In these circumstances there will have been an infringement of a work, but the copyright owner's commercial exploitation of the work is deemed not to have been unduly harmed.

Fair dealing, s29

Fair dealing covers non-commercial research or private study, criticism, review and reporting current events. If the part taken is not substantial, then there is no infringement of copyright and no need to rely on the permitted acts. You must consider the number, extent and proportions of any quotations. Long extracts and short comments may be unfair. If the use made of them is for comment, criticism or review, that may be fair dealing. If they are used for a rival purpose, they may be unfair. But it must be a matter of impression of whether it would seriously prejudice the commercial value of the copyright work.

EXAM TIP

Note that an injunction will rarely be granted if the defendant has an arguable defence of fair dealing. This is to protect freedom of speech. Highly relevant to the press and politics.

Research or private study, s29

This applies to the original works. The research must be for non-commercial purposes. There is a requirement that a sufficient acknowledgement be made, the name of the author and title of the work. The research must be to facilitate the person's own research, not another's. So providing study notes for others would not be included.

Criticism, review and reporting current events, s30

The section applies to all original works plus performances. The criticism or review must be accompanied by a sufficient acknowledgement. It will only be available if the work has been made available to the public. The criticism or review does not need to be the only purpose for using the work, provided it was a significant purpose. The criticism does not have to be of the work itself but can be directed at another work. A TV programme (the work) can be used to comment on the use of 'chequebook' journalism (another work).

In reporting current events, the event involved does not have to be recent but must comment on other events which are of current interest. So an old video of Princess Diana could be used to comment upon a current event such as her inquest. It does not apply to photographs, and an acknowledgement does not need to be made if impractical to do so.

Chapter summary:
Putting it all together

☐ Can you tick all the points from the revision checklist at the beginning of this chapter?

☐ Take the **end-of-chapter quiz** on the companion website.

☐ Test your knowledge of the cases below with the **revision flashcards** on the website.

☐ Attempt the essay question from the beginning of the chapter using the guidelines below.

☐ Go to the companion website to try out other questions.

Answer guidelines

See the essay question at the start of the chapter.

Points to remember when answering this question

■ First note that, under section 16(3) CDPA, infringement requires that the relevant restricted act has to be carried out in relation to the whole or a substantial part of the work.

■ Refer to cases such as *Hawkes* v *Paramount* to note that it is the quality of the part taken rather than its quantity that is important.

■ Mention that when testing for infringement, comparison should be made between the part taken and the claimant's work rather than the defendant's work.

■ Deal with Lord Hoffmann's statement – you could usefully introduce cases such as *Kenrick* v *Lawrence* here which is a good example of what he was thinking about.

Make your answer stand out

■ It would help to mention something about the policy of copyright protection. For example, if ideas are expressed with little detail, there is the difficulty of deciding whether there has been copying, if denied. Also, copyright would be in danger of protecting ideas rather than expression.

FURTHER READING

Heath-Saunders, A. 'It's a fair copy: the defence of fair dealing in cases of copyright infringement' [2005] June, Corporate Briefing 8.

Sims, A. 'The public interest defence in copyright: myth or reality?' [2006] 6 EIPR 335.

Spencer, M. 'Vagueness in the scope of copyright' [2005] LQR 657.

Stephens, K. 'Copyright: non-textual infringement' [2006] 5 CIPA Journal 356.

4
Confidentiality

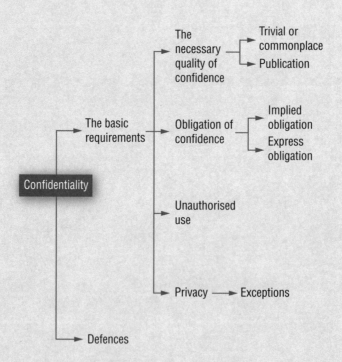

A printable version of this topic map is available from www.pearsoned.co.uk/lawexpress

Revision checklist

Essential points you should know:

- [ ] What is required for information to be regarded as confidential.
- [ ] Who is bound by confidential material.
- [ ] Status of employees with confidential material and trade secrets.
- [ ] Public interest defences.
- [ ] Privacy, Human Rights Act and the public interest.

Introduction

If you say that you will keep a secret, then you must.

If you acquire secret information in confidence you may use it only for the purposes for which it was given to you. Confidential information may be personal, commercial, industrial or governmental. Such information is not restricted to the written or spoken word but may also include images and ideas. This is a very difficult area of law and although an obligation of confidence may arise in contract, much is implied by the principles of equity. It is judge-made law and although benefiting from flexibility, many of the cases contradict each other. However, for information to be regarded as confidential it must have the necessary quality of confidence about it. No one will be prevented from using truthful information or reverse engineering products that are already in the public domain. You cannot impose a secret on someone. In addition you cannot stop an employee using their skill and know-how in order to gain employment but you may obtain an injunction to prevent them from divulging trade secrets or acting in breach of their duty of fidelity. Although there is no fundamental right of privacy in English law, the law of confidence, combined with the Human Rights Act 1998 and with Articles 8 and 10 of the Council of Europe Convention on Human Rights and Fundamental Freedoms, can protect the right of privacy subject to disclosure in the public interest.

Assessment advice

Essay questions

Essay questions on this topic may well ask you to follow developments in this flexible area of law. This could involve discussion of commercial secrets and the development of the 'springboard' doctrine with the subsequent decision that rather than granting an injunction, damages are an adequate remedy. You may also be asked to analyse the changing nature of private information due to the advent of the Human Rights Act.

Assessment advice

Problem Questions

Problem questions may well involve difficult areas, such as when an innocent third party receives confidential information without realising its confidential nature or when eavesdropping occurs. There may also be a problem that involves the 'kiss and tell' type of story or where an ex-partner or ex-employee sells the story or writes a book depicting their time in the company/employment of a celebrity.

Sample question

Could you answer this question? Below is a typical problem question that could arise on this topic. Guidelines on answering the question are included at the end of this chapter, whilst a sample essay question and guidance on tackling it can be found on the companion website.

PROBLEM QUESTION

Liz is a jazz singer. She has had considerable success but has always been a private person and has not encouraged publicity. For many years she was in daily contact with Olive, with whom she went to school. Olive was her best friend and confidante. Olive helped Liz overcome depression after she divorced her husband due to his adultery, and it was Olive who helped her come to terms with the fact that she had Parkinson's disease (a progressive neurological condition that affects walking, talking and writing). Olive accompanied Liz on all the singing tours she made between 1992 and 2005, eating together every evening, meeting all her friends and generally sharing her life. In 2004 the relationship between the two women grew strained, culminating in a very bad argument. They have not spoken for two years. Liz has discovered that Olive has written a book about their friendship which is about to be published. Liz became aware of the book following enquiries she made after she was startled by one photographer taking a photograph of her walking along the street and another climbing onto the wall of her garden so that he could take photographs of her sunbathing.

Both photographs of Liz have been sold to newspapers, which are about to publish them. Olive says that the book is not about Liz but about her own life during the period of 1992–2005 and Liz cannot prevent its publication.

Advise Liz on whether she can prevent the publication of the book and the photographs.

■ The basic requirements

Coco v ***A N Clark (Engineers) Ltd*** [1969] RPC 41, ChD

Concerning: Basic requirements for liability

Facts

Marco Paolo Coco designed a moped engine. He entered into negotiations with Clark to manufacture the engine but these negotiations broke down. No contract was involved. Clark produced a similar moped engine, which Coco unsuccessfully claimed was based on his engine.

Legal principle

(1) The information must have the necessary quality of confidence about it.
(2) The information must have been imparted in circumstances imposing an obligation of confidence.
(3) There must be an unauthorised use of that information to the detriment of the party communicating it.

The necessary quality of confidence

Trivial or commonplace

In order to be held to be confidential, information must not be trivial or commonplace, in the public domain or too vague. It does not have to be particularly special information, and simple things such as lists of customers can be regarded as confidential. Trade secrets however are given far stronger protection. There is unfortunately no legal definition of trade secrets.

Faccenda Chicken Ltd v ***Fowler*** [1986] 1 All ER 617, CA

Concerning: An ex-employee taking sales information

Facts

An employee left his employment with know-how concerning the fresh chicken trade of his employer. He started up in competition using this know-how.

Legal principle

Trivial information, easily accessible information and employee know-how are not protected as trade secrets. Trade secrets are so confidential that there is a duty even without a contractual agreement to keep them secret after the end of the employment relationship.

Other issues are the nature of the employment; would the employee usually handle confidential information? The nature of the information itself: would it be easily available to the public? Did the employer stress the confidential nature of the material, and could the information be easily isolated from other material the employee was free to use?

KEY DEFINITION

Trade secret. A trade secret is information that would cause real harm if it were disclosed to a competitor and the owner had limited its dissemination.

Some duties of confidence, such as that of an employee and employer, although expressed in a contract of employment, are also implied by law. The implied duty of ex-employees is far less onerous than that of present employees and covers only trade secrets, unless protected by a specific contractual term.

Problem area: Implied duty of employee to keep employer's secrets

There is a balance required between the need of employees to work using the know-how and experience gained through their employment and the need for the employer to protect their sensitive information from being dispersed to rivals.

To determine whether the information is to be regarded as a trade secret one must look at the nature of the employment, the nature of the information and whether the employer impressed upon the employee the confidentiality of the information. In addition, whether the information can be easily isolated from other information the employee is free to disclose are important issues to be considered.

Publication

If information is in the public domain it will no longer be confidential and its use can no longer be prevented. This is unless the person whose conscience was fixed by the confidence put the information in the public domain themselves. If this is the case they may be prevented by an injunction from using the information to the detriment of the owner for a period of time. This is called the 'springboard' doctrine and is intended to prevent such a person benefiting from their own wrong. It may however be felt that damages are a more appropriate remedy than an injunction.

Obligation of confidence

The information must have been imparted in circumstances importing an obligation of confidence. The party receiving the information must have their conscience fixed in equity. This can either be by contract, by oral agreement, or implied by law. The test can be subjective – was it assumed by the parties that the disclosure was in confidence? – or objective – would other reasonable people assume the information had been imparted in confidence? If no one would reasonably think that the circumstance could give rise to a confidence, then it will not.

Problem area: Eavesdropping

It is uncertain if an obligation arises in such circumstances, as the information has not been imparted in circumstances importing an obligation of confidence, as required in *Coco* v *Clark.*

Implied obligation

By using such methods as encryption when selling goods you are making information difficult to access or reverse-engineer, as well as letting people know that you do not want them to access your secret information. Does this mean that their conscience is fixed in equity? This can be problematic, for without a contractual agreement there is no consent on the behalf of the purchaser and a confider cannot impose an obligation of confidence upon another.

EXAM TIP

It is worth pointing out that as technology improves it is much easier for people to gain access to confidential material but that the circumstances importing an obligation of confidence may not exist. Make sure you stress the flexibility offered by the law of confidence. We can see the benefits of it being able to adapt, demonstrated in *Douglas* v *Hello! (No 6)* where it was accepted that taking photographs surreptitiously was a breach of confidence.

KEY CASE

Michael Douglas v *Hello! Ltd* [2006] QB 125, CA

Concerning: Whether unauthorised photographs were taken in breach of a duty of confidence

Facts
A photographer, despite heavy security, surreptitiously took photographs of a celebrity wedding. The photographs were published in the magazine *Hello!* and the celebrities sued the magazine for breach of confidence.

Legal principle
Making it clear that photographs should not be taken, together with strict security measures, can give rise to a duty of confidence.

Keep in mind that this was not a commercial situation but a case of private information where the parties had a reasonable expectation of privacy. The fact that the photographer had not agreed to be bound was irrelevant as he knew that the information was reasonably regarded by the couple as confidential.

Express obligation

Restrictive covenants can be included in the contract of employment and these will protect the employer even after the employment relationship has ended. They should not however be drafted too widely in either length or width, or the courts will find them unenforceable. The court will not rewrite a clause on behalf of the employer. Neither will they uphold a covenant that goes beyond the protection necessary for trade secrets; for instance in an attempt to prevent competition or prevent the ex-employee using his skill and knowledge.

Problem area: Third party

If a third party receives information knowing it to be confidential or in circumstances where a reasonable person would assume that the information is confidential, they too will be bound. If however they only later discover the confidential nature of the information they may be under an obligation from the time they become aware of its nature and their conscience will then become fixed. However, if the innocent third party has not agreed to be bound it would seem not to comply with the guidance in *Coco* v *Clark*, that the information must have been imparted in circumstances imposing an obligation of confidence.

Unauthorised use

The use must be detrimental to the party that communicated it. This can be economic damage or where there is harm to a person's social standing.

REVISION NOTE

Confidential information is extremely important in the pre-filing stage of a patent application. Refer to Chapter 5 on patentability.

Privacy

There is no right of privacy in English law but since 1998 Art 8 of the Human Rights Act has established that everyone has a right to respect for their private and family life, their home and correspondence. There is however a conflicting right in Art 10, the right to freedom of expression, and these rights can be at variance.

KEY DEFINITION

Private information. Information or conduct, the disclosure of which would be highly offensive to a reasonable person of ordinary sensibilities.

Campbell v *Mirror Group Newspapers* [2004] 2 All ER 995, HL

Concerning: Misuse of private information and whether disclosure was in the public interest

Facts

Naomi Campbell, a 'supermodel', had claimed that she was not addicted to drugs. The *Mirror* newspaper published an article describing the treatment she was undergoing at Narcotics Anonymous and a photo of her coming out of a Narcotics Anonymous meeting.

Legal principle

By a majority decision the court decided that a role model can be exposed for hypocrisy, consequently drug treatment after denial of addiction was open to exposure. However, there is still a 'reasonable expectation of privacy' and the photograph was not necessary in order to demonstrate that she had lied.

There must be a balance between a right to privacy and the right to freedom of expression. There is some information that has an obvious 'reasonable expectation of privacy'. It must of course be personal, the claimant must not have intended to share it with the general public, and such private information will include information on health, sexual orientation, intimate relationships and finances. The information will not be private if it is generally accessible or if it relates to a criminal act.

Problem area: Photographs

In *Campbell* the photographs taken on the street were held to be private and confidential. This seems to be a very great extension to matter which can be regarded as secret.

Exceptions

There are exceptions under the Human Rights Act in respect of, *inter alia* :

■ National security
■ Prevention of crime
■ Protection of rights or freedoms of others.

■ Defences

There are defences of justification, or fair comment. Confidential information will not be protected where there has been wrongdoing or inappropriate behaviour. An important defence to an accusation of breach of confidence is that the publication was made in the public interest. The breach was necessary to allow the wrongful behaviour to be discovered. Consequently the public interest in the revelation of the information outweighs the plaintiff's right to confidentiality. But remember, just because information is of interest to the public does not mean it is in the public interest to know it. Also, some confidential relationships such as doctor/patient or solicitor/client are very important and disclosure would rarely be accepted as being justified. If however the disclosure was felt to be necessary the information must only be disclosed to the appropriate authorities, never the newspapers.

FURTHER THINKING

The second requirement in *Coco* v *Clark* that the information must have been imparted in circumstances imposing an obligation of confidence has been in some cases circumvented in recent years. However, this does not seem to be universal. There also seems to be a difference between quality of confidence and the treatment of commercial and private information. Private information is protected if there is a reasonable expectation of privacy, but should commercial information be protected if a person knew or ought to have known that it was confidential in nature? (The answer is no.)

For a discussion of this see T. Aplin, 'Commercial confidences after the Human Rights Act' [2007] EIPR 411.

Chapter summary:
Putting it all together

☐ Can you tick all the points from the revision checklist at the beginning of this chapter?

☐ Take the **end-of-chapter quiz** on the companion website.

☐ Test your knowledge of the cases below with the **revision flashcards** on the website.

☐ Attempt the problem/question from the beginning of the chapter using the guidelines below.

☐ Go to the companion website to try out other questions.

Answer guidelines

See the problem question at the start of the chapter.

Points to remember when answering this question

■ Liz can claim breach of confidence and an injunction for the book and at least one of the photographs.

■ Traditionally, under *Coco* v *Clark* confidential information needed:
  (1) the necessary quality of confidences, not trivial, commonplace or in the public domain
  (2) imparted in a situation imposing an obligation of confidence
  (3) unauthorised use made by the party under the obligation.

■ With private information after *Campbell* and *Douglas* it is no longer necessary to have a confidential obligation imposed. There is now an assumption that if information is private it is also confidential.

■ Information about health matters such as depression will be regarded as private, as would a husband's adultery, unless Liz had public rows with her husband about it.

■ A confidential duty now arises where a person knows or ought to know that there was a reasonable expectation of privacy, so the information in the book would be private and confidential.

■ Once the information is held to be private the courts will then balance Articles 8 and 10 HRA.

■ Olive claims the book is about her life and she has a right to freedom of expression (Art 10 HRA). The court is likely to hold that Olive's experiences were only a reflection of Liz's life and Liz's right to privacy outweighed any right of Olive's.

■ In *Campbell* photographs were held to be private and an injunction was granted but here we must ask would Liz really have a reasonable expectation of privacy in walking along a public road, unlike in the walled garden?

Make your answer stand out

■ Stress that the fact that Liz did not talk about her life in public, that she had not exposed herself to media interest and that she was not held out as a role model is very important. She had not behaved hypocritically as had Naomi Campbell. Just because she is famous does not mean the public have a right to know all about her.

FURTHER READING

Brazell, L. 'Confidence, privacy and human rights: English law in the twenty-first century' [2005] 11 EIPR 405.

Lang, J. 'The protection of commercial trade secrets' [2003] 10 EIPR 462.

5
Patentability

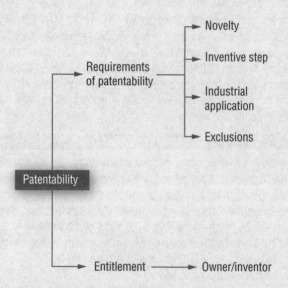

A printable version of this topic map is available from www.pearsoned.co.uk/lawexpress

Revision checklist

Essential points you should know:

- [ ] What is meant by 'novelty'.
- [ ] What will destroy novelty.
- [ ] What an enabling disclosure is.
- [ ] What constitutes an inventive step.
- [ ] What material a skilled person should take into account when assessing inventive step.
- [ ] What inventions are capable of industrial application and which are excluded.
- [ ] Who is entitled to claim to be the inventor or owner of an invention.

Introduction

Ideas by themselves are not protectable but in some circumstances 'ideas' can be developed into a successful patent application.

Patents are granted for new, non-obvious product or process inventions that have an industrial application and which have not been excluded from patentability. On payment of a fee a patent gives the owner a monopoly in a particular territory, enabling them to exploit the invention exclusively for a period of up to 20 years. Although the inventor benefits from the patent in that he can work, sell or license it, society also benefits because not only is innovation encouraged but the invention will eventually fall into the public domain.

Assessment advice

There may be a question that incorporates patentability in your examination. Novelty may include issues of confidentiality and the date of filing. Inventive step may involve what appears to be a routine development rather than an inventive step. The issue of industrial application may need some discussion about the actual construction of the claim. Sometimes the facts seem to be very scientific, which can appear daunting but remember, you are not being asked to understand the science, you are being asked to apply the law. If you do this clearly and appropriately you should gain a good mark.

It is very important to remember when talking about patents that there are significant policy issues involved in this area of law. There is an underlying intention that society will benefit in two ways: by the innovation that will be encouraged by a period of monopoly given to the owner of the patent, then ultimately because the invention will become available to be exploited for the use of all. However, there are exclusions to the grant of a patent. These exclusions are also made for policy reasons.

Sample question

Could you answer this question? Below is a typical essay question that could arise on this topic. Guidelines on answering the question are included at the end of this chapter, whilst a sample problem question and guidance on tackling it can be found on the companion website.

ESSAY QUESTION

Being such a strong monopoly right, it is not surprising that patent rights are tempered by numerous exceptions to infringement in the form of defences. A person sued for an alleged infringement of a patent has several and varied escape routes. *Discuss.*

■ Requirements of patentability

> **KEY STATUTE**
>
> ### *Section 1 Patents Act 1977*
>
> 'A patent may be granted ... if
>
> a) the invention is new
> b) it involves an inventive step
> c) it is capable of industrial application
> d) it is not excluded'

A new invention means new to the public, so that secret use will not destroy novelty. An inventive step is something that is not obvious to someone skilled in the art. 'Capable of industrial application' means that no matter how clever it is, unless it is a product or process which has a function there can be no patent granted. Finally, no patent will be granted for certain excluded inventions.

Novelty

> **KEY STATUTE**
>
> ### Section 2 Patents Act 1977
>
> An invention shall be new if it does not form part of the state of the art. The state of the art comprises all matter (whether a product, a process, information about either, or anything else) which has at any time before the priority date been made available to the public (whether in the United Kingdom or elsewhere) by written or oral description, by use or in any other way. The state of the art shall also comprise matter contained in an application for another patent which was published on or after the priority date of the invention at issue.

Problem area: State of the art

To avoid being regarded as part of the state of the art the invention must not have been made available to the public in any way, anywhere in the world, at any time before the priority date. If it has it will have become part of the state of the art and thus novelty will have been destroyed. There are problems in what constitutes the 'use' that needs to be made of the invention to amount to making it available to the public.

If something has been available to the public in the past, even if in a far-off country and a very long time ago, it will not be regarded as new for the purposes of section 1 of the Patents Act. However, assuming it is indeed new, if you reveal your invention before the filing date in any way, by telling people (or even one person) about it, by writing an article in a journal or by giving a talk at a conference, novelty will be destroyed and you will be unable to obtain a patent unless your disclosure was made in circumstances of confidence.

REVISION NOTE

When considering novelty, remember that disclosures made in confidence will not become part of the state of the art. You should refer to Chapter 4 on confidentiality in relation to non-disclosure agreements.

KEY CASE

Lux Traffic Controls Ltd v *Pike Signals Ltd* [1993] RPC 107 ChD

Concerning: What use amounts to disclosure to the public

Facts

It was claimed that a temporary traffic signal was not 'new' because it had been made available to the public in a paper, by oral disclosure and by the use of a prototype which had been tested in Somerset.

Legal principle

A prior publication must contain clear and unmistakable directions to do what the patentee claims to have invented; a signpost will not suffice. Where prior use is concerned there is no need for a skilled person to actually examine the invention as long as they were free in law and equity to do so and if a skilled person had seen it they would have been able to understand what the inventive concept was.

KEY DEFINITION

The skilled person. The skilled person is an unimaginative person, or team of uninventive people, with the common general knowledge available to a person in the field at the date of filing. They will only think the obvious and will not question general assumptions.

Note that a skilled person is needed to decide if there has been disclosure, for they understand the state of the art in the area of the invention. They do not actually have to see or touch the invention for it to have become available to the public, but they must have been free in law or equity to have done so.

KEY CASE

Synthon v *SmithKline Beecham plc* (No 2) [2006] RPC 323, HL

Concerning: The differing roles of the skilled person in relation to the concepts of disclosure and enablement

Facts

This was an appeal to the House of Lords by Synthon to revoke SmithKline's patent for an anti-depression drug. The application was based on the disclosure of Synthon's own flawed earlier patent application. SmithKline's patent was found to be invalid for lack of novelty based on s2(3) of the Patent Act 1977.

Legal principle

What is regarded as part of the state of the art includes things disclosed to a skilled person which, if performed, must infringe the patent. To decide if there was an enabling disclosure it is assumed that the skilled person would be willing to conduct trial and error experiments to get the invention to work.

FURTHER THINKING

Section 2(3) is intended to prevent double patenting so that a prior, even unpublished, patent application destroys novelty. It would be worth your while in a problem question where there had been an unpublished patent application by another to quickly explain that you understand that this is why this section is applicable only to the issue of novelty and not to the question of obviousness. *Synthon* v *SmithKline Beecham Plc* is an important case in this area and is discussed by Sharples & Curley (see Further Reading). They explain that to anticipate a patent the prior publication must contain clear and unmistakable directions to do what the patentee claims to have invented; a signpost needing trial and error experimentation will not suffice. Reference to this article would display wider reading and allow you to gain a depth of understanding on this issue.

Any disclosure which can anticipate an invention must be viewed by the unimaginative skilled reader at the time of the publication. It must not be viewed with hindsight taking into account the present invention. The prior disclosure must not just be an indication, a possibility or a signpost but *must* lead to the present invention. However, the skilled man may use his unimaginative skill and knowledge plus trial and error experiments to attempt to make the prior disclosure work. Consequently the skilled man in *Lux Traffic Controls* (above) could experiment by driving up to the traffic lights at different speeds in order to see how to trigger the change of lights. If by this experimentation he is *bound* to discover the inventive concept, it has been disclosed. Enablement is different. With enablement the skilled man must, from what was disclosed, be able to make the invention work, using unimaginative trial and error experiments etc. not just understand what it is.

EXAM TIP

Using headings when dealing with issues such as disclosure and enablement will make sure that you do not confuse them. Your reader will also understand that you know they are two separate concepts.

Inventive step

KEY STATUTE

Section 3 Patents Act 1977

'An invention shall be taken to involve an inventive step if it is not obvious to a person skilled in the art, having regard to any matter which forms part of the state of the art ...'

To obtain a patent the invention must not only be new but it must also involve some invention or creative concept. This prevents a monopoly being created over things that are common general knowledge and should therefore be available for all to use.

Problem area: Inventive step

It is important to stress that an inventive step is not merely an obvious extension to what has gone before. It requires either the addition of a new idea to the existing stock of knowledge, or doing a new thing, achieving a goal or solving a problem. It is not possible to give a statutory definition of what constitutes an inventive step but guidelines have been established by the courts in the *Windsurfing* case and you must be able to discuss these in detail.

Windsurfing International Inc v *Tabur Marine (CB) Ltd* [1985] RPC 59, CA

Concerning: A structured way of approaching the problem of whether an invention is obvious to a person skilled in the art

Facts

The claimant had a patent for a windsurfing board and took action against the defendant for infringement of the patent. The defendants claimed that the patent should be revoked for invalidity as the invention had been anticipated in 1958 by a boy aged 12 who had used a similar sailboard while on a short holiday.

Legal principle

The court must identify the inventive concept of the patent, assume the mantle of the skilled but unimaginative person with common general knowledge of the time, identify the difference between the cited matter and the invention, then ask whether those differences constitute steps which would have been obvious or whether they require invention.

The inventive step must not have been obvious to a skilled man at the time of the invention as the next step to take, neither should it have been obvious to him to undertake trials to that end.

A member of the public would not be a useful comparator. Many people, especially with the advanced technologies, would find it all a mystery and would never understand how the invention worked or find it obvious, even if it were explained to them in great detail. The existence of a long-felt want could indicate that the solution was not obvious. Large sales however may be due to other reasons, such as fashion or a better method of manufacture, rather than the inventiveness of this particular product or process.

EXAM TIP

It has been accepted that the *Windsurfing* test is only to be regarded as guidance because it is not appropriate for as-yet undiscovered technologies. However, it is worth showing your examiner that you are aware that failure to apply these principles in court would probably result in an appeal.

Industrial application

> **KEY STATUTE**
>
> ### Section 4 Patents Act 1977
>
> '... an invention shall be taken to be capable of industrial application if it can be made or used in any kind of industry, including agriculture.'

The most important issues related to industrial application will be dealt with under the heading of exclusions. Other than that the invention must have some sort of use. But remember it does not have to be better, cheaper or quicker than what came before; it just needs to be different.

Exclusions

> **KEY STATUTE**
>
> ### Sections 1 and 4A Patents Act 1977
>
> Excluded from patentability are discoveries, scientific theories, mathematical methods, aesthetic creations, schemes, rules or methods for performing a mental act, playing a game, doing business, a program for a computer or the presentation of information *'as such'*. Also excluded are patents which are regarded as contrary to public policy or morality, methods of treatment of the human or animal body by surgery or therapy or of diagnosis practised on the human or animal body.

Some of the exclusions can be justified on the grounds of lack of technical effect. Many are abstract and related to information rather than inventions and more appropriately protected by copyright. Some are regarded as discoveries or knowledge that should be available for all to use, such as mathematical methods and the treatment or diagnosis of the human or animal body. However, treatment implies that there is some sort of illness or disease. Although such treatment is denied patent protection it is perfectly acceptable to patent a drug which is used in the treatment. In addition, there are further exclusions which are more controversial, such as those relating to business methods and in particular to computer programs.

Problem area: Excluded matter

Although all these areas are excluded it is important to keep in mind that the tests for industrial application under section 4 and patentability under section 1 are separate. It is also important to remember that many of the things which are not to be regarded as inventions are abstract or intellectual and are more suited to being protected by copyright. Some are excluded for public policy reasons. There is a feeling that methods of treatment should be available for all doctors or vets to use to treat their patients, even though the drugs used in those treatments may be granted a patent. A monopoly is regarded as necessary to make sure that the research and development cost of drugs companies are recouped to enable them to continue with further innovation.

Aerotel/Macrossan Patent Application [2006] EWHC 705 CA

Concerning: The exclusion from patentability of business methods and computer programs

Facts

This concerns two joined cases. Aerotel succeeded in their application regarding a new telephone system where a pre-payment code could be used to make a call from any telephone to the company's exchange, while Macrossan's application failed having been held to be a method of doing business. It merely programmed a machine to ask appropriate questions in order to decide which documents should be used to incorporate a company.

Legal principle

To decide if this was excluded subject matter, being a computer program or business method 'as such', one must: (1) properly construe the claim; (2) identify the actual contribution (what has the inventor really added to human knowledge?); (3) ask whether it falls solely within the excluded subject matter; (4) check whether the actual or alleged contribution is actually technical in nature. The presence of a technical effect is only to be considered if the invention has passed the first three steps.

FURTHER THINKING

Computer programs and business methods are highly significant as commercial assets and in both Japan and the USA they are regarded as patentable. There is an obstacle in the way of their patentability in Europe and there has been an ongoing debate about whether, although this may be to the advantage of small software business in the UK, it is to the disadvantage of the economy as a whole. In their article 'Test clarified for UK software and business method patents: but what about the EPO?', Cook and Lees review the EPO (European Patent Office) and UK case law and explain how, although there has been an attempt by the EPO towards harmonisation, the approach to coordinating the patenting of computer programs in the EU has not yet been achieved.

Each IP course is likely to approach the issue of the patentability of computer software differently. Some courses may look at the historical progression of the debate within Europe while some may take an international contemporary comparative approach. You must follow the guidelines in the syllabus provided for you by your lecturer and ensure that you concentrate on the areas dealt with on your particular course.

EXAM TIP

Showing that you are aware of the 'bigger picture' is likely to please your examiner. So explain that even though the aim of both the EPO and UKIPO is for European harmonisation, they have different views on the patentability of computer programs. Keep in mind, when answering any question in this area, that exclusions are made for policy reasons and not because there is a coherent reason for them. Why should doctors be prevented from patenting their methods of treatment while drugs companies are able to monopolise life-saving drugs? Also offer practical advice stressing that the first advice that should be given to any prospective patentee is to keep his invention confidential. If in doubt, say nowt!

■ Entitlement

There is a difference between the inventor and the proprietor or owner of a patent. Anyone may apply for a patent but the inventor must be identified in the application. A patent will only be granted to someone who is entitled to it, the inventor, their employer or someone to whom the invention has been transferred.

Owner/inventor

Patents are very valuable rights and often more than one person is involved in their creation. The first step in deciding who is entitled to be regarded as the inventor is to identify the inventive concept, and only then can you work out who was responsible for taking the inventive step. If it was created in the course of employment the employer will usually be entitled to ownership of the invention but compensation may be available to the employee if the patent is of outstanding benefit to the proprietor.

Most inventions are uncontroversial as to ownership and are made in the course of employment by people employed to invent. Disputes arise either where there is no expectation of invention on the employee's part but the employment contract attempts to claim ownership of all an employee's intellectual output, or where the inventor is in a managerial position within the company. Directors owe fiduciary duties to their company. They must always put the company's interests before their own and will be held to be under a special obligation to work in the best interests of the company. There is however a grey area in relation to lower managers where it is uncertain whether they owe such a special obligation or not.

IDA Ltd v *University of Southampton* [2006] RPC 567, ChD

Concerning: Right to be considered the inventor

Facts

A university professor invented a cockroach trap which caused poisoned electronically charged talcum powder to attach to the legs of the insects. Having read about the invention Mr Metcalf, although not knowing that the powder became attached to the insects, correctly suggested to the professor that magnetic powder might be more efficient than an electro-statically charged powder. The professor applied for a new patent using magnetic powder. It was decided that Mr Metcalf was the inventor after a dispute arose as to who had the right to the patent.

Legal principle

To be considered as an inventor a person does not have to be skilled in the art in question: all that is required is that the person provided the inventive aspect to the patent. Having common general knowledge was not enough to be inventive. Routine trials are not inventive; the question is whether they had contributed the heart of the invention.

Remember that although one person may be responsible for the inventive step, if it is impossible to separate individual contributions you may have joint inventors.

Chapter summary:
Putting it all together

☐ Can you tick all the points from the revision checklist at the beginning of this chapter?

☐ Take the **end-of-chapter quiz** on the companion website.

☐ Test your knowledge of the cases below with the **revision flashcards** on the website.

☐ Attempt the problem question from the beginning of the chapter using the guidelines below.

☐ Go to the companion website to try out other questions.

Answer guidelines

See the essay question at the start of the chapter.

Points to remember when answering this question

▪ Briefly explain the requirements of patentability, and what are not to be regarded as inventions.

▪ Although asking about exclusions the question specifically refers to computer programs.

▪ Do not merely describe what the exclusions are.

▪ Explain the inclusion of 'As such' after the list of exclusions. Advise they are not excluded totally but only if the patent is for the excluded thing, such as a scientific theory, itself.

▪ Although the quote states that in many cases these exclusions can be justified on the grounds of lack of technical effect or technical contribution, you should point out that the exclusions are regarded as non-patentable for different policy reasons and are not linked in any way. They are not all abstract and they do not all lack a technical character.

▪ Explain that the deemed comparative disadvantage that Europe suffers due to the ease with which the US and Japanese can patent business methods and computer software ensures that these are the most controversial exclusions.

▪ Briefly outline the historical development mentioning the 'technical contribution', the 'technical effect' and 'any hardware approaches'.

▪ Examine the joined cases *Aerotel/Macrossan* (see Further Reading) and apply the current UK four-step approach, discussing the result of that application.

Make your answer stand out

▪ Show awareness that even though the two are supposed to be harmonised there are different and conflicting approaches of the EPO and UKIPO. See Further Thinking above.

▪ Explain that the joined cases *Aerotel/Macrossan* have led the UKIPO to issue a new practice direction. Indicating how it will apply the judgment will show that you are aware of the important consequences of this case.

▪ You could conclude by asking if there are any serious reasons why computer programs should not be patented. Is it because copyright protection is available? Is it pure policy due to pressure from powerful interest groups?

FURTHER READING

Cook, W. and Lees, G. 'Test clarified for UK software and business method patents: but what about the EPO?' [2007] 3 EIPR 115.

Sharples, A. and Curley, D. 'Experimental Novelty: *Synthon* v *SmithKline Beecham*' [2006] 5 EIPR 308.

6

Patent infringement

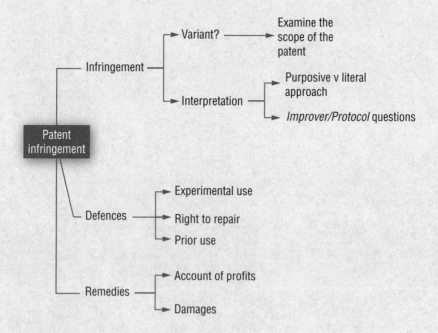

A printable version of this topic map is available from www.pearsoned.co.uk/lawexpress

Revision checklist

Essential points you should know:

- [ ] What acts amount to an infringing act.
- [ ] What knowledge is required of the infringer.
- [ ] How the scope of the invention is determined.
- [ ] The function of the reader skilled in the art.
- [ ] What is meant by a variant having a material effect.
- [ ] The time at which the reader skilled in the art should consider the claim.
- [ ] The view the skilled reader should take about the language of the claim.
- [ ] Defences.
- [ ] Remedies.

Introduction
Understanding infringement

A patent proprietor has a right to prevent all third parties for making or using the patented product or process without his consent.

Infringement occurs if a patented product or process is exploited within the UK without the patentee's consent. A patent has to be in force in order to be infringed, and commonly a defendant in infringement proceedings will try to establish that the patent is invalid. If successful, any infringement proceedings will come to a halt and the claimant will have lost their patent permanently.

Bar a claim of invalidity, if a patent is merely copied infringement proceedings may be quite straightforward. Problems arise where the invention has not been taken in its entirety but some feature has been changed or an additional feature included. Before it can be decided whether a patent has been infringed the invention must be defined. This entails looking at what has been specified in the claim as interpreted by the description and drawings. The interpretation of the specification has caused debate within the EU. In granting the strong monopoly right of a patent it is necessary to achieve a balance between fair protection of the patentee and reasonable certainty for third parties.

Sample question

Could you answer this question? Below is a typical problem question that could arise on this topic. Guidelines on answering the question are included at the end of this chapter, whilst a sample essay question and guidance on tackling it can be found on the companion website.

PROBLEM QUESTION

Wendy invented and patented 'Dobbinsafe', an air-cooled horse exercise boot. The specification states that the boot is intended to prevent damage to a horse's leg caused by exercise-induced strain or by external striking. The boot is formed of a leg-embracing collar secured around a horse's leg and the surface of the boot includes at least one air intake, exit outlets and channels connecting the intake and outlets to allow coolant air or fluid to penetrate the surface and pass from one part of the boot to the other, hitting the horse's leg as it gallops. Wendy is aware that an Italian product, 'Ridesure', is being marketed in the UK. This horse exercise boot includes an outer layer which is made up of small holes throughout with an inner layer of foamed permeable material. This will allow air to flow into the boot and reach the leg when the horse is galloping. Wendy feels that the Ridesure boot infringes her patent.

Advise Wendy on the likelihood of an infringement action succeeding and what remedies are available if her patent is found to have been infringed.

Infringement

Infringement. Infringement occurs if a validly patented product or process is exploited within the UK without the patentee's consent and with no defence available.

Remember that if infringement proceedings are commenced it is common for the defendant to attempt to have the patent revoked. If successful there will be no valid patent and therefore no infringement.

Problem area: The facts

The facts of cases in this area can seem very confusing to non-scientists but the law itself is on the whole quite clear, although there is a conflict between the interpretation of the English courts and those of some other European countries.

KEY STATUTE

Section 60(1) and (2) Patents Act 1977

A person infringes a patent for an invention if in the UK and while the patent is in force they, without the consent of the proprietor, make, dispose of, offer to dispose of, use, import or keep a patented product. Where the invention is a process, a person infringes a patent if they use or offer it for use when they know, or it is obvious to a reasonable person in the circumstances, that its use in the UK without the consent of the proprietor would be an infringement of the patent. Infringement also occurs where, if the invention is a process, a person disposes of, offers to dispose of, uses, imports or keeps any product which was obtained directly by means of that process. In addition a person also infringes a patent if in the UK they supply or offer to supply the means, or essential element of the invention, for putting the invention into effect when they know, or it is obvious to a reasonable person in the circumstances, that those means are suitable for putting, and are intended to put, the invention into effect in the UK.

EXAM TIP

Be careful about the culpability of the infringer to determine if damages are available. Do not forget that the knowledge required of the infringer is different depending on whether you are talking about a product or a process. There is no requirement of knowledge for infringement of a product; liability is strict unless there is a defence available. For infringement of a process it must be obvious to a reasonable person that the patent is being infringed. Although it is unlikely that there will be an examination question concerning the section 60(2) act of 'supplying the means' you should still be aware that it exists.

What if there is a variant?

If an invention has been copied exactly the only problems that may arise will relate to the validity of the patent and any defences. However, if there is a variation this may still give rise to a successful infringement action.

Examine the scope of the patent

Section 125(1) of the Patents Act 1977 is in effect the same as Article 69 of the European Patent Convention and states that the invention is regarded as what is specified in the claim as interpreted in the description and any drawings.

> **KEY STATUTE**
>
> **Section 125(1) Patents Act 1977**
>
> An invention for a patent for which an application has been made or for which a patent has been granted shall, unless the context otherwise requires, be taken to be that specified in a claim of the specification as interpreted by the description and any drawings contained in that specification. The extent of the protection conferred by a patent shall be determined accordingly.

How is this to be interpreted?

The protocol on the interpretation of Article 69 states that it should not be interpreted by the strict, literal meaning of the wording used in the claims, the description and drawings being employed only for the purpose of resolving any ambiguity. Neither should it be interpreted using the claims only as a guideline. A position between these extremes should be taken which combines a fair protection for the patentee with a reasonable degree of certainty for third parties.

Problem area: But what about the interpretation of the claim?

The protocol concerns the interpretation of Article 69, not the interpretation of claims. Article 69 EPC states that the claim must be construed in order to decide what is the monopoly right of the patentee. But we are still left with the question of how the courts should interpret the claim.

The purposive v literal approach

KEY DEFINITION

Purposive approach. The purposive approach looks at the purpose or reason for making the claim.

The literal approach is the traditional approach taken by lawyers and favoured in the UK. It provides great certainty to third parties. Any deviation from the words in the claim will mean there is no infringement. The purposive approach looks at the purpose or reason for making the claim. Deviation from the words used can be quite wide but still fall within what may have been envisaged as intended to be claimed by the patentee. This gives wider protection to the patentee but adds uncertainty to third parties who may or may not find themselves having infringed the patent.

KEY DEFINITION

Person skilled in the art. The person skilled in the art is an unimaginative person, or team of uninventive people, with the common general knowledge available to a person in the relevant field at the date of filing. They will only think the obvious and will not question general assumptions.

KEY CASE

Catnic Components Ltd v *Hill & Smith Ltd* [1982] RPC 183, HL

Concerning: the interpretation of the claim and whether a minor variation would avoid a successful infringement action

Facts

The claimant had a patent for a lintel which stated that the rear face was vertical. The defendant was held to have infringed the patent having made a similar lintel but with a rear face which was 6 degrees from vertical.

Legal principle

A patent specification should be given a purposive construction aimed at the skilled workers in the field rather than a purely literal interpretation designed for lawyers.

In order to take a balanced approach one must ask whether a person, skilled in the art, would understand that strict compliance with a particular word or phrase was intended by the patentee to be an essential requirement of the invention. If so, any variant that did not comply would fall outside the claim regardless of whether it had any effect. If the variant did have a material effect, there would be no infringement.

EXAM TIP

Show that you are aware that a purposive interpretation can lead to greater protection for the patentee but uncertainty for the third party who having read the specification may infringe unintentionally. Although a fair balance is needed you could observe that the patentee has the opportunity to draft his claim as widely as he chooses and if he fails to do so he only has himself to blame.

The *Improver/Protocol* questions

The *Catnic* case demonstrated that using the purposive interpretation 'vertical' would easily be seen by the skilled person as being intended to include 'slightly off vertical'. There was a greater problem of interpretation however if the variant of a rubber rod was used rather than a helical spiral as specifically mentioned in the claim.

KEY CASE

Improver Corp v *Raymond Industrial Ltd* [1991] FSR 223, CA (Hong Kong)

Concerning: guidance on how to interpret a claim when there is an equivalent

Facts

The claimant had a patent for the 'Epilady', a device claiming use of a helical spring for removing hair from arms and legs. The defendant had a similar device called 'Smooth & Silky' which performed the same function but used a rubber rod rather than a spring. This was held to be outside the claim.

Legal principle

The court should ask itself the following three questions:

(1) Does the variant have a material effect on the way the invention works? If yes, the variant is outside the claim (and does not infringe). If no?

(2) Would this (i.e. that the variant had no material effect) have been obvious at the date of publication of the patent to a reader skilled in the art? If no, the variant is outside the claim. If yes?

(3) Would the reader skilled in the art nevertheless have understood from the language of the claim that the patentee intended that strict compliance with the primary meaning was an essential requirement of the invention? If yes, the variant is outside the claim.

We are left with having to decide what a person skilled in the art would have understood the patentee to have used the language of the claim to mean. Remember however that the *Improver/Protocol* questions merely provide guidance in trying to address this problem (see *Kirin-Amgen* below). The courts do not intend to give the patentee more than can be found within the claim.

Problem area: High technology

The *Improver/Protocol* questions may not be helpful in a rapidly developing high technology field such as genetic engineering. Whether a patentee should have worded their claim to include a rubber rod in addition to a spring may be an obvious and reasonable expectation. A patentee in a rapidly developing field would have to word their claim in a way that included the new, as yet unheard-of, technology (see *Kirin-Amgen*). Surely an impossibility!

Kirin-Amgen Inc v *Hoechst Marion Roussel Ltd* [2005] RPC 169, HL

Concerning: whether the *Improver* questions could be used to decide if the skilled person could envisage how a new technology would work

Facts

The claimants, KA, were the proprietors of a patent which used DNA technology in a host cell to artificially produce a hormone EPO. This increased the production of red blood cells in the kidney, thereby increasing iron uptake. It was found that the defendant had not infringed this patent by making EPO using a variant of the process. It would not in this case have been obvious to a person skilled in the art that the variant worked in the same way as the invention, nor would they regard the claim as being sufficiently general to be intending to cover unknown technology at the time the claim was drafted.

Legal principle

The *Improver* questions are merely a guide to determine what the person skilled in the art would have understood the patentee to be using the language of the claim to mean. It is the principle laid down in *Catnic* that must be followed.

EXAM TIP

Highlight that despite the purposive approach it is still up to the inventor to specify the extent of his monopoly. If he has not claimed something it is not up to the court to rewrite the specification. He may have left something out for a sensible reason such as avoiding prior art or the accusation of lack of inventive step. Remind your reader that the patents and their claims are meant to be statements made by the patentee to the relevant public, and their meaning and effect should be clear from reading the document.

When asking the second *Improver* question it is easy to see that it should have been obvious that a helical spiral could have the same effect as a rubber rod with slits. It is far less easy to see how a patentee could have intended to cover something in their claim that had not yet been invented at the filing date. It could not have been obvious to the skilled person as they had no concept of its existence and so the second *Improver* question is not appropriate in this sort of circumstance. It is necessary, as stated in *Kirin-Amgen*, to fall back on *Catnic* and ask what the person skilled in the art would have understood the patentee to be using the language of the claim to mean. If that language can be construed to cover things not yet in existence then there can be infringement; if not there will be no infringement.

FURTHER THINKING

The article by Curley & Sheraton, 'The Lords rule in AMGEN *v* TKT' clearly follows the development of the interpretation of Article 69 discussing the *Catnic, Improver* and *Kirin-Amgen* cases. They explain that in *Amgen* Lord Hoffmann concludes that the *Catnic* approach to construction which led to the *Improver* questions was 'precisely in accordance with the protocol' but that the *Improver* questions are merely guidelines useful in interpreting the law. Hoffmann, they state, also makes it plain that although it is not possible to extend the scope of the patent it is acceptable to take due account of any element which is equivalent to an element specified in the claims. This would be an important part of the background of facts known to the skilled man which would affect what he understood the claim to mean.

■ Defences

You must always pause to consider whether a defence is available, even if you quickly discount the possibility. The exceptions to infringement are set out in s60(5) (a–f). In effect they all amount to innocent infringement. Defences include when an invention has been worked, or serious preparations to work it have been made before the priority date, or where ships, aircraft, etc. are for a limited time (even if frequently) or accidentally in the UK. There are also defences aimed at farmers: an unlikely topic for an examination question, and where there is exhaustion of rights under European Community law. It must always be kept in mind that if an infringement action is started the defendant may in return attack the validity of the patent, most commonly attempting to have it revoked for lack of novelty or inventive step.

Experimental use

There are some things that are no threat to the commercial exploitation of the patent and may indeed benefit the furtherance of knowledge in our society. These things are therefore specifically allowed.

Section 60(5) Patents Act 1977

'An act which, apart from this subsection, would constitute an infringement of a patent for an invention shall not do so if –

(a) It is done privately and for non-commercial purposes
(b) it is done for experimental purposes relating to the subject-matter of the invention'

There is a defence of private use but the use must be for the person's own use *and* not for any commercial purposes.

Auchincloss v *Agricultural & Veterinary Supplies Ltd* [1997] RPC 649, CA

Concerning: What acts amounted to experimental use for s60(5)(b)

Facts

The patent was for a dry, water-soluble biocidal composition which the claimant alleged had been infringed by the manufacture of an experimental sample which had been made for and supplied to MAFF by the defendant in order to obtain official approval.

Legal principle

Trials to discover something unknown or to test a hypothesis are regarded as legitimate experiments but trials carried out to reaffirm what is already known or to show that a product works or to obtain official approval are not.

In addition a monopoly should not be allowed to inhibit scientific developments and as experimental use does not pose a threat to the patent holder it is allowed. Experimentation must be on the invention itself, it cannot be use of the invention for experimental purposes on something else.

EXAM TIP

Experimentation is often illegitimately undertaken during the life of a patent in order to swiftly enter the market as soon as the patent expires. It would make your answer stand out if you included some mention of available remedies such as post-expiry injunctions or 'springboard relief'. The courts have granted injunctions to run after the expiry of the patent in order to prevent a person selling articles made during the subsistence of the patent, thus putting them in the position they would have been in if they had not 'jumped the gun'. However, point out that damages may be a more appropriate remedy.

Right to repair

KEY STATUTE

Section 60(1)(a) Patents Act 1977

A person infringes a patent for a product invention if he *makes* the product.

We can see that there may be a fine line between making a product, which is an infringement, and repairing a product, which is allowed. Which it is, is a question of fact.

KEY CASE

United Wire Ltd v *Screen Repair Services (Scotland) Ltd* [2001] RPC 439, HL

Concerning: The existence and scope of the right of repair

Facts

The claimant was the proprietor of a patent for sifting screens, a mesh screen bound to a frame, which was used to recycle drilling fluid. The mesh frequently wore out and the defendant reconditioned the screens by applying new meshes to the existing frames. H of L held that the screen was the combination of the frame and meshes and had ceased to exist when the meshes were removed. This was held not to be repair but to be manufacture and hence an infringement.

Legal principle

It is a matter of fact and degree but genuine repair of a product does not constitute making the product and is therefore not an infringement.

Prior use

KEY STATUTE

Section 64(1) Patents Act 1977

'Where a patent is granted for an invention, a person who in the United Kingdom before the priority date of the invention –

(a) does in good faith an act which would constitute an infringement of the patent if it were in force, or

(b) makes in good faith effective and serious preparations to do such an act, has the right to continue to do the act or, as the case may be, to do the act, notwithstanding the grant of the patent; but this right does not extend to granting a licence to another person to do the act.'

This defence will only be available where the prior use was not only in good faith but also secret, for otherwise the use would have anticipated the patent. Section 64 however only provides a defence and there is no right to licence others to do the prior act.

FURTHER THINKING

It is always worthwhile bearing in mind that patent protection aims to balance the benefit to society by encouraging innovation and the spread of knowledge with the monopoly given to the patentee. Section 64 is part of that balance and is intended to safeguard the existing commercial activity of a person in the UK which may have been overtaken by the subsequent grant of a patent. It is not however meant to allow him to expand into other areas at the expense of the patentee. Hence, although it depends on the circumstances, 'effective' must be more than just preparation to do an act; the infringing act must be about to be done. For a clear explanation of s64 and why the problem might arise see Cohen and Davies, 'Section 64 of the UK Patents Act 1977: Right to continue use begun before priority date'.

◼ Remedies

The remedies available for infringement of a patent are found in section 61 and include an injunction, a discretionary remedy, an order for delivery up or destruction, damages, an account of profits, and a declaration that the patent is valid and has been infringed by the defendant.

EXAM TIP

When discussing these remedies it would be worth explaining that they are a non-exhaustive list and could be expanded. Do not forget that damages and an account of profits are alternatives and may not, by section 61(2), both be awarded in respect of the same infringement. So do not ask for a remedy that is not available. However, do not omit to mention that the court has discretion to award damages in lieu of, or in addition to, an injunction.

Account of profits

Bear in mind that the purpose of an account of profits is not to punish the defendant but to prevent his unjust enrichment. They are an alternative to damages but are rarely asked for in patent cases because of the complexity in quantifying them.

Damages

Damages are often based on the value of the royalties that the infringer would have paid had he taken a licence. Otherwise damages will be based on normal considerations of causation and remoteness but you would not normally be expected to discuss these issues in any depth unless you are specifically asked to do so.

EXAM TIP

There will often be a few words at the end of a problem question asking you to consider what remedies will be available to the parties. Be aware that 'innocent' infringers may escape some of the remedies. Damages are not available if the defendant can prove that, at the time of the infringement, he was not aware and had no reasonable grounds for supposing that the patent existed.

REVISION NOTE

Make sure that you keep in mind the validity issue covered in Chapter 5 when answering any question on infringement, as it is common for the defendant in such a case to claim that the patent is invalid for some reason.

Chapter summary:
Putting it all together

☐ Can you tick all the points from the revision checklist at the beginning of this chapter?

☐ Take the **end-of-chapter quiz** on the companion website.

☐ Test your knowledge of the cases below with the **revision flashcards** on the website.

☐ Attempt the problem question from the beginning of the chapter using the guidelines below.

☐ Go to the companion website to try out other questions.

Answer guidelines

See the problem question at the start of the chapter.

Points to remember when answering this question

- To decide if there has been infringement you must first determine what is the monopoly claimed by Wendy?

- Section 125 says you must look at the claim, description and any drawings. Here the claim is for the 'air intake, exit outlets and channels connecting the intake and outlets to allow coolant air or fluid to penetrate the surface, pass from one part of the boot to the other hitting the horse's leg as it gallops'.

- In *Catnic* it was stated that the purposive construction should be taken.

- Guidance is given on this approach in the three *Improver/Protocol* questions.

- In *Kirin–Amgen* it was stated that the question should be what the skilled person in the art would have understood the patentee to be using the language of the claim to mean.

- You could assume that the skilled person is knowledgeable in the field of exercise boots for horses.

- The question to be posed here is: Would the person skilled in the exercise boots field understand that in Wendy's boot the air or fluid was to be guided to the horse's leg through the outlets and channels alone, or would they understand that she was claiming that the air was to flow freely throughout any permeable material?

- If you decide on the former there is no infringement, and if on the latter there could be infringement if there are no defences.

- When discussing remedies you should mention that an injunction is the most common remedy sought and that although an account of profits is available it is an alternative to damages.

Make your answer stand out

▮ Stress that you understand that taking the literal approach to the interpretation of the claim would mean that any derivation from the words of the claim will not give rise to infringement while adopting the purposive approach would give Wendy much stronger protection. You could also point out that although the *Improver* questions are only guidance, failing to ask these questions may give rise to an appeal.

FURTHER READING

Cohen, S. and Davies, I. 'Section 64 of the UK Patents Act 1977: Right to continue use begun before priority date' [1994] EIPR 239.

Curley, D. and Sheraton, H. 'The Lords rule in *Amgen* v *TKT*' [2005] EIPR 27.

7
Design law

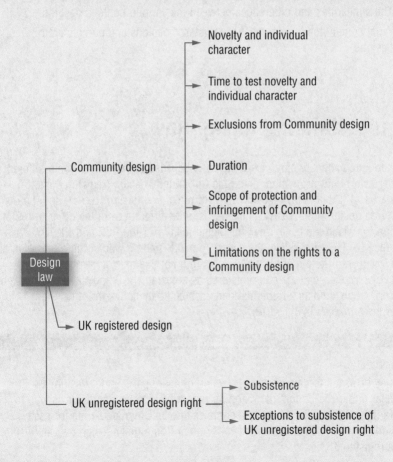

- Community design
  - Novelty and individual character
  - Time to test novelty and individual character
  - Exclusions from Community design
  - Duration
  - Scope of protection and infringement of Community design
  - Limitations on the rights to a Community design
- UK registered design
- UK unregistered design right
  - Subsistence
  - Exceptions to subsistence of UK unregistered design right

Design law

A printable version of this topic map is available from www.pearsoned.co.uk/lawexpress

Revision checklist

Essential points you should know:

☐ The rules for subsistence of the Community design and the UK registered design

☐ Definitions of 'design', 'product' and 'complex product'

☐ What novelty and individual character mean

☐ Key concepts such as 'informed user', 'immaterial differences' and 'commonplace'

☐ The requirements for subsistence of the UK unregistered design right

☐ Key concepts such as 'commonplace', 'must-fit' and 'must-match'

☐ The similarities and differences between the various rights in designs

☐ What constitutes infringement of registered designs and unregistered designs

Introduction
Understanding design law

Design law often appears complex to students because there are four main different forms of design right protection, being the Community design (registered and unregistered, RCD and UCD respectively), UK registered design (UKRD) and the UK unregistered design right (UDR). The latter is quite different from the other forms of protection for which the basic rules for registrability (for the RCD and UKRD) or subsistence (UCD) are basically the same. To make matters worse, there may also be some overlap with trade mark law and copyright. For example, a non-trivial and distinctive computer icon may be registered as a design (RCD and UKRD), protected by the UCD, registered as a trade mark and protected by copyright. It will not, however, be protected by the UDR.

Assessment advice

Essay questions

You may be asked to discuss the protection of spare parts under design law, in particular under-the-bonnet parts and parts that have to be a particular shape to restore the original appearance of a complex article. Other areas ripe for essay questions include the rationale for two forms of Community design (registered and unregistered).

Assessment advice

Problem questions

Problem questions on Community designs are likely to focus on registrability (RCD) or subsistence (UCD) and infringement. You may be asked to apply concepts such as the 'informed user', 'overall impression' and 'design freedom' to particular cases. For the UK unregistered design right, the effect of the permitted act under section 51 of the Copyright, Designs and Patents Act 1988, effectively suppresses copyright protection in design documents and models.

Sample question

Could you answer this question? Below is a typical essay question that could arise on this topic. Guidelines on answering the question are included at the end of this chapter, whilst a sample problem question and guidance on tackling it can be found on the companion website.

ESSAY QUESTION

The existence of the UK's unregistered design right compromises the scheme of protection set out in the Community Design Regulation.

Critically discuss this statement with reference to subsistence of the rights and limitations to them.

REVISION NOTE

Try thinking of a number of different products or articles and consider which of the design rights might apply to them, assuming that they are new and distinctive.

■ Community design

There are two forms of Community design, one subject to registration (RCD), the other informal (UCD). The basic requirements for both are the same (apart from the date at which novelty and individual character is tested).

KEY DEFINITION

Community design. A community design has a unitary character and has equal effect throughout the Community. It may only be registered, transferred, surrendered, declared invalid or its use prohibited in relation to the entire Community.

The design must conform to the key definitions of 'design', 'product' or 'complex product', it must be new and have individual character (and not fall within the exclusions; see later).

KEY STATUTES

Article 3 Community Design Regulation

(a) 'design' means the appearance of the whole or a part of a product resulting from the features of, in particular, the lines, contours, colours, shape, texture and/or materials of the product itself and/or its ornamentation;

(b) 'product' means any industrial or handicraft item, including *inter alia* parts intended to be assembled into a complex product, packaging, get-up, graphic symbols and typographic typefaces, but excluding computer programs;

(c) 'complex product' means a product which is composed of multiple components which can be replaced, permitting disassembly and re-assembly of the product.

Article 4(1) Community Design Regulation

A design shall be protected by a Community design to the extent that it is new and has individual character.

Novelty and individual character

A design is new if no identical design (including a design with features which differ only in immaterial details) has been made available to the public.

A design has an individual character if the overall impression it produces on an *informed user* differs from the overall impression produced on such a user by any design which has been made available to the public.

KEY CASE

Crown Confectionery Co Ltd's design (No ICD000000388, 20 September 2005), OHIM

Concerning: Novelty of a pretzel-shaped design

Facts

An application for invalidity was made in respect of a design to be applied to pretzel-shaped biscuits.

Legal principle

The design did not differ from existing designs except in immaterial details, being the familiar pretzel shape and only having some lines drawn across the surface of the design.

The 'informed user' is not the same as the 'average consumer' of trade mark law. The informed user has experience of similar products and will be reasonably discriminatory and able to appreciate sufficient detail to decide whether or not the design under consideration creates a different overall impression. The degree of design freedom is taken into account.

Pepsico Inc's design (No ICD000000172, 20 June 2005) OHIM

Concerning: Individual character and design freedom

Facts

This design in question was for a disk having annular rings or corrugations applied to a promotional item for games. There was a challenge to the validity of the design. The design was declared invalid.

Legal principle

The informed consumer would be familiar with promotional items and would pay more attention to graphical elements rather than minor variations in shape. Furthermore, although there were some constraints to design freedom, these were to do with cost and safety and, otherwise, there was ample design freedom. Thus, the informed user may focus on certain aspects of a design and design freedom should be looked at in the round, and some constraints may be present without significantly reducing the overall design freedom. Reasons for design freedom may be a relevant factor to be taken into account.

Time to test novelty and individual character

The time when a design has been made available to the public differs between the RCD and the UCD. This is further complicated as the RCD provides for the priority of earlier applications elsewhere for up to six months.

■ RCD relevant date is the date of filing the application, or earlier priority date if there is one.
■ UCD relevant date is the date the design itself is first made available to the public.

There is a 12-month period of grace for the RCD so, for example, the designer may market products to the design during that period before filing the application to register.

'Under-the-bonnet' parts which are not seen during normal use of a complex product are not considered to be novel or to have individual character.

Problem area: 'Made available to the public' and period of grace

It can be tricky working out dates for novelty and individual character where the period of grace and priority date are involved. The figure below shows three possibilities (there are more).

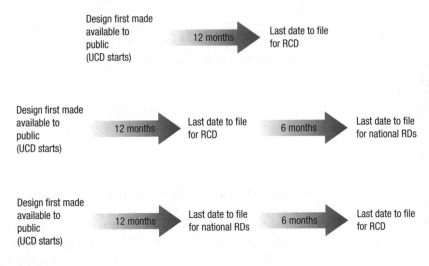

Exclusions from Community design

■ Features dictated by technical function.
■ 'Must-fit' features (except in respect of modular systems which are protectable in principle).
■ Designs contrary to public policy or morality.
■ 'Must-match' spare parts used to restore the original appearance of a complex product.

The last exception is easily missed as it is buried away in Article 110 of the Community Design Regulation (transitional provisions). The exception is subject to review but is likely to remain. Note that the presence of excepted features does not prevent protection of other features. For example, a design of a teapot with an overall shape which is well-known but which has a new design of spout having individual character may be protected. The scope of protection will be limited accordingly.

KEY CASE

3M Innovative Properties Co's designs (No ICD000000040, 14 June 2004) OHIM

Concerning: The scope of the exclusion of features dictated by function

Facts

The design in question was in respect of a swab on a stick used to dispense antiseptic to the skin.

Legal principle

Where part of a design is dictated by function, the informed user will concentrate on the other aspects of the design to determine whether the design has individual character.

Duration

- RCD – 5 years from the date of filing. It may then be renewed for further periods of 5 years up to a maximum of 25 years.
- UCD – 3 years from the date the design was first made available to the public.

For the purposes of the UCD in determining the start of the 3 years, it is made available to the public when it is published, exhibited, used in trade or otherwise disclosed in such a way that, in the normal course of business, these events could reasonably have become known to the circles specialised in the sector concerned within the Community. No account is taken of disclosure by a person under an express or implied duty of confidentiality.

Problem area: Duration of unregistered community design

The unregistered Community design lasts for three years from the date the design was first made available to the public within the Community. Unlike copyright and the UK unregistered design, the duration is not tied in to the end of the relevant calendar year. So, for example, if an unregistered Community design was first made available to the public on 12 September 2008, it comes to an end on 12 September 2011. However, because of the period of grace, an application to file for registration of the design can be made up to and including 11 September 2009.

Scope of protection and infringement of Community design

The scope of protection for a Community design resembles the test for individual character in that it is a question of whether the alleged infringing design, from the perspective of the informed user, does not produce a different overall impression compared with the protected design. Design freedom is taken into consideration.

Article 10 Community Design Regulation

(1) The scope of protection conferred by a Community design shall include any design which does not produce on the informed user a different overall impression.

(2) In assessing the scope of protection, the degree of freedom of the designer in developing his design shall be taken into consideration.

The registered Community design gives the rightholder a monopoly right which is infringed by a person using it without the rightholder's consent. Use, in particular, includes making, offering, putting on the market, importing, exporting or using a product in which the design is incorporated or applied, or stocking such a product for those purposes.

For the unregistered Community design, it is required that the use in question results from copying the protected design. This also applies during the period of deferred publication where the design is registered but publication has been deferred. An applicant to register a Community design can defer publication by up to 30 months from the filing date, hence delaying the payment of the publication fee.

Procter & Gamble Co v *Reckitt Benckiser (UK) Ltd* [2008] FSR 8, CA

Concerning: Individual character

Facts

This was a case on the alleged infringement of a registered Community design applied to a spray container for air fresheners.

Legal principle

To escape infringement, a design did not have to be 'clearly different' and it was sufficient if it differed in a way that the informed user was able to discriminate. The notional informed user would be fairly familiar with design issues and was more discriminating and careful than the average consumer of trade mark law. What mattered was what stuck in the mind of the informed user when he viewed the products, not after he had viewed them, and consequently, 'imperfect recollection' had a limited role to play. Where design freedom was limited, smaller differences could create a different overall impression. The trial judge erred by applying a 'stick in the mind' test rather than a 'what would impress now' test and his finding that there was infringement was reversed.

Limitations on the rights to a Community design

The rights to a Community design (registered or unregistered) do not extend to the following acts:

- Acts done privately and for non-commercial purposes
- Acts done for experimental purposes
- Reproduction for citation or teaching in accordance with fair practices without unduly prejudicing the normal exploitation of the design, providing the source is mentioned
- Acts in respect of the repair of ships or aircraft temporarily in the Community.

Furthermore, the doctrine of exhaustion of rights applies to Community design. For the registered Community design, there are also provisions in relation to prior use commenced in good faith before the filing date (or priority date, if there is one) or where serious and effective preparations have been made to commence use, providing such use did not involve copying the registered design.

Problem area: Right to continue prior use

The right to continue prior use is similar to the equivalent mechanism for patents, with one major difference. Because of the period of grace, it is possible for products incorporating a design or to which a design has been applied to be put on the market for a period of up to 12 months before filing an application to register a design as a Community design. Because of this there has to be an additional requirement, and the right to continue prior use applies only where the design in question has not been copied by the person claiming the right to continue prior use. Of course, if the design has been copied during that period of grace the owner of the design will be able to bring an action based on his unregistered Community design.

FURTHER THINKING

David Bainbridge, 'The registration as designs of computer icons, graphical user interfaces and webpages', *The Computer Law and Security Report* (2006), 22(3), 218.

Explores how computer icons and graphical user interfaces may be registered as Community designs and also be protected by the unregistered Community design in addition to protection under the UK registered design. This is a 'sea change' from the position prior to harmonisation of registered designs and the introduction of the Community design.

■ UK registered design

The UK registered design was modified substantially as a result of the Directive harmonising registered design law throughout the Community. As a result, the basic principles, such as subsistence and the scope of the rights of the owner, are virtually identical to those for the registered Community design except, of course, references to the Community are to the UK.

The UK Registered Designs Act 1949, as amended, does of course have specific provisions as to ownership and remedies. For example, where the creation of a design occurs under a commission for money or money's worth, the person commissioning its creation will be entitled to be the proprietor of the design. The remedies for infringing a UK registered design are the same as for infringement of a Community design. There are also provisions for delivery up, disposal of infringing articles, etc.

KEY STATUTE

Section 24A(2) Registered Designs Act 1949; regulation 1A(2) Community Designs Regulations 2005, as amended

In an action for infringement [of a Community design] all such relief by way of damages, injunctions, accounts or otherwise is available to him [to the holder of a Community design] as is available in respect of the infringement of any other property right.
[wording relevant to the Community design]

There is also a remedy for groundless threats of infringement proceedings which also applies in respect of a Community design (registered and unregistered). There is an equivalent remedy for the UK unregistered design right.

■ UK unregistered design right

The UK unregistered design right was introduced by the Copyright, Designs and Patents Act 1988 in an attempt to overcome the problems of protection of functional designs by means of copyright in drawings showing the designs, as highlighted in *British Leyland Motor Corp* v *Armstrong Patents Co Ltd* [1986] 2 WLR 400.

EXAM TIP

In problem questions on registered designs, always be prepared to consider whether there is unregistered design protection (whether the UK unregistered design right or unregistered Community design). Although the UK unregistered design right is very different from Community design and from the UK registered design, it may be present in respect of many designs protected in other ways.

Subsistence

The following key statutory provisions indicate just how different the UK unregistered design right is from other forms of design protection. It should be studied and compared to the basic requirements for subsistence of Community design. It is clear that originality is first considered in a copyright sense before looking at whether the design is commonplace.

KEY STATUTE

Section 213(1), (2) and (4) Copyright, Designs and Patents Act 1988

(1) Design right is a property right which subsists in accordance with this Part in an original design.

(2) In this Part 'design' means the design of any aspect of the shape or configuration (whether internal or external) of the whole or part of an article.

...

(4) A design is not 'original' for the purposes of this Part if it is commonplace in the design field in question at the time of its creation.

KEY DEFINITION

Commonplace. The word 'commonplace' was new to English law when introduced by a Directive protecting semiconductor topographies. There are a number of judicial statements, none of which are entirely satisfactory. They include:

'... any design which is trite, trivial, common-or-garden, hackneyed or of the type which would excite no peculiar attention in those in the relevant art is likely to be commonplace'

'What really matters is what prior designs the experts are able to identify and how much those designs are shown to be current in the thinking of designers in the field at the time of creation of the design in question'.

It is important to note, however, that a design which has become very familiar does not necessarily become 'commonplace'. For example, if a design is applied to an article made by one manufacturer which sells in large numbers, that does not necessarily mean it is commonplace.

Exceptions to subsistence of UK unregistered design right

KEY STATUTE

Section 213(3) Copyright, Designs and Patents Act 1988

(3) Design right does not subsist in –
(a) a method or principle of construction,
(b) features of shape or configuration of an article which –
(i) enable the article to be connected to, or placed in, around or against, another article so that either article may perform its function, or
(ii) are dependent upon the appearance of another article of which the article is intended by the designer to form an integral part, or
(c) surface decoration.

The first exception, methods or principles of construction, is unlikely to be relevant in the vast majority of cases. The exceptions in section 213(3)(b)(i) and (ii) are often referred to as the 'must-fit' and 'must-match' exceptions. Surface decoration is also excepted, this being the proper subject matter of copyright. An example of surface decoration is a willow pattern applied to a dinner plate.

KEY CASE

Dyson Ltd v *Qualtex (UK) Ltd* [2006] RPC 31, CA

Concerning: Various aspects of design right including the scope of the 'must-fit', 'must-match' and surface decoration exclusions

Facts

The defendant supplied duplicate spare parts (pattern parts) for the claimant's vacuum cleaners. The claimant sued on the basis of unregistered design rights subsisting in the design of the parts of its vacuum cleaners.

Legal principle

The 'must-fit' exclusion does not mean that the articles have to physically touch. A clearance between them, if it allows one article to perform its function, may be within the exclusion. The exclusion may apply where the two articles are designed sequentially, one after the other.

For 'must-match' exclusion it is design dependency which is important. The more room there is for design freedom, the less likely the exception will apply.

The reason for the surface decoration exclusion was because it was protected by copyright. Surface decoration could be applied to a two-

KEY CASE

dimensional article or three-dimensional article or to a flat surface of a three-dimensional article. Surface decoration was not limited to something applied to an existing article and it could come into existence with the surface itself. Surface decoration could itself be three-dimensional, such as beading applied to furniture. However, a feature having a function, such as ribbing on the handle of a vacuum cleaner, was unlikely to be surface decoration. This had a function of helping provide grip.

A design must qualify for protection and may qualify by virtue of the design, the commissioner (if commissioned) or employer (if created by an employee). It may also qualify by virtue of the person who first markets articles to the design in the European Community if it does not otherwise qualify. These provisions are mirrored in those concerning first ownership of the design right.

Chapter summary:
Putting it all together

Answer guidelines

See the essay question at the start of the chapter.

Points to remember when answering this question

■ The question asks for a critical discussion so your answer should go beyond the mere descriptive.

■ It would be useful to first set out the relevant provisions in the Community Design Regulation whilst seeking to reflect on the underlying policy for the scheme under the Regulation.

■ Remembering that the question is concerned with the scheme of protection under the Community Design Regulation, this requires consideration of the rules for registrability (or subsistence in the case of the unregistered Community design), the scope of protection, the rights of the owner and limitation of those rights.

■ Identify and discuss the equivalent aspects of the UK unregistered design right, noting that it is quite different from the Community design, and critically analyse and comment on to what extent and how they conflict with the scheme under the Community Design Regulation.

■ An example of this is that an unregistered design may be protected for only three years under the Community design yet the same design *may* be protected in the UK by the unregistered design right for up to 15 years (bearing in mind of course that the overlap between the two forms of protection is by no means complete because of the different rules for subsistence and, for the UK unregistered design right, qualification requirements).

■ Other examples include the fact that additional damages may be available for infringement of the UK unregistered design right and there are no limitations to the rights equivalent to those for Community design, for example, teaching, experimentation and repairing ships and aircraft.

Make your answer stand out

▪ Having addressed the conflicts between the Community design and the UK unregistered design right, construct and support an argument about whether the UK unregistered design right ought to be repealed, for example, on the basis that it is now unnecessary or confuses the issues of protection of designs.

▪ It might impress an examiner to note that the Community design is not without its problems, for example the protection of graphic symbols and typefaces which may also be protected by copyright law. Unless such designs are registered, giving monopoly protection, there is little point in the Community design for them. Furthermore, as the period of protection for the unregistered Community design commences when first made available to the public the UK approach of basing duration on the end of the calendar year of creation is arguably more certain.

FURTHER READING

Bainbridge, D. 'Groundless threats and the internet' [2007] 3 CLSR 282.

Carboni, A. 'Design validity and infringement: feel the difference' [2008] 3 EIPR 111.

Michaels, A. 'The end of the road for pattern spare parts? *Dyson Ltd* v *Qualtex (UK) Ltd* ' [2006] 7 EIPR 396.

8
Trade mark registrability

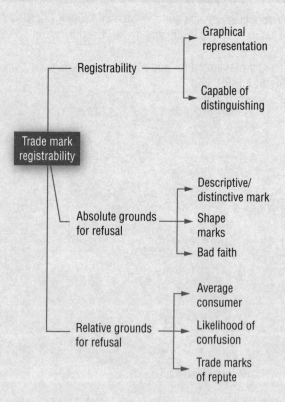

A printable version of this topic map is available from www.pearsoned.co.uk/lawexpress

Revision checklist

Essential points you should know:

- [ ] The meaning of a sign
- [ ] How a sign can be represented graphically
- [ ] The absolute grounds for refusal of registration
- [ ] The relative grounds for objection
- [ ] What is an identical or similar mark and what are identical or similar goods or services
- [ ] The definition of consumer
- [ ] How the consumer will perceive the marks and goods
- [ ] How the likelihood of confusion is assessed
- [ ] What will amount to a mark with a reputation
- [ ] What constitutes without due cause, unfair advantage and detriment.

Introduction
Understanding trade marks

The purpose of a trade mark is to distinguish the goods or services of one undertaking from those of other undertakings.

Trade marks are a badge of origin and may have great economic value. They are the most harmonised of the IP rights in the European Union. The Trade Marks Act 1994 (TMA) implemented the European Community's First Council Directive to approximate the trade mark laws of member states. A trade mark is registered under a class of good or services initially for a period of ten years but it can then be renewed every ten years as long as it is being used in the appropriate class. You must use it or lose it. It is a property right which arises on registration and can be licensed or sold. It is enforceable by the owner or licensee of the right. However, not only can a trade mark be used to help a business in furtherance of its trade but it can also protect consumers from being deceived into buying the wrong or even counterfeit goods or services.

Assessment advice

Essay questions

You may be asked to discuss the policy reasons for refusing the registration of a trade mark. This will entail dealing with the absolute grounds of refusal with discussion on the distinctive rather than descriptive nature of a trade mark. This ground prevents proprietors from monopolising marks that should be free for all to use. You will also have to examine the relative grounds where registered marks are protected against the use by rival traders dealing in the same or similar goods or services, leading to confusion in the mind of the consumer. There is no confusion needed where extra protection is given to an existing sign which has a reputation. Such signs are vulnerable to free riding and detriment may occur if a subsequent similar mark is registered even for dissimilar goods. This gives extremely strong protection to the proprietor of the right. The reasons for this additional protection may need to be analysed.

Problem questions

Whether a mark can be represented graphically sounds like a simple question but difficulties can arise when you are attempting to register colour, shape, smell and sound marks. Although there may not always be a full problem question on this area it may well come into the discussion of any issues surrounding registrability and there may be an essay question on the problems associated with registering such marks.

Sample question

Could you answer this question? Below is a typical problem question that could arise on this topic. Guidelines on answering the question are included at the end of this chapter, whilst a sample essay question and guidance on tackling it can be found on the companion website.

PROBLEM QUESTION

Toys Ltd has created a new night-time toy of unusual shape which could only be described as an alien hedgehog. The toy when warmed by the heat of a child's body gives off a chocolate smelling sleeping gas which causes the child to fall into an uninterrupted night's slumber. The hedgehog shape provides a considerable surface area so that a sufficiently large dose of the gas can escape even if the toy is being tightly cuddled. The toy is a luminous puce colour.

Advise Toys Ltd as to the likelihood of success in registering the colour, smell and shape of their toy.

■ Registrability of trade marks

Trade mark – fundamental attributes. A mark will only be registered as a trade mark if it is a sign, if it can be represented graphically and if it is capable of distinguishing one trader's goods or services from those of another.

We know from section 1 of the TMA that a sign can consist of words, designs, letters, numerals or the shape of goods or their packaging. So the shape of a bottle or a person's name can all be regarded as signs and on the face of it are registrable. We are then told that even though they qualify as a sign they will only be registrable if they are *also* capable of graphical representation and *also* capable of distinguishing one trader's goods from those of another.

Graphical representation

Problem area: Graphical representation

There are problems with the graphical representation of colour, sound, taste and smell marks. A mark must be advertised in the *Trademark Journal* so that other traders know what marks are registered so they can avoid infringing them. If the representation of the marks is not certain, clear, precise and durable, traders cannot know if they are infringing another's mark. With regard to smell marks in particular it may be impossible to even ascertain what the trade mark is despite detailed descriptions and chemical formulae being provided. Such marks are unlikely to be accepted.

KEY CASS

Shield Mark BV v *Joost Kist* [2004] RPC 315, ECJ

Concerning: Whether a sound mark can be represented graphically

Facts

This was a failed application 'to register the first 9 notes of Beethoven's "Für Elise" 'along with the musical stave depicting the notes plus the designation 'the crowing of a cock', also described using the Dutch word Kukelekuuuuuu .

Legal principle

Representation will only be accepted if clear, precise, self contained, easily accessible, intelligible, durable and objective.

In *Shield Mark* the musical notes and stave were found to be insufficiently concise. If there had been more detail provided so that in addition to the notes the stave was divided into measures with a clef, rests and accidentals this would have been sufficiently precise to be registered. The legal principle that the graphical representation of a mark must be clear, precise, etc. is also applicable to determining whether colour, smell, taste and shape marks are adequately graphically represented.

Capable of distinguishing

Once you have established that a mark is capable of graphical representation the next requirement that must be met for section 1 is that it must be capable of distinguishing. More explanation of this is found under section 3 of the Trade Marks Act 1994 or Article 3 of the Directive.

■ Absolute grounds for refusal

Section 3(1)(a-d) Trade Marks Act 1994, Art 3 (1)(a-d) Directive on the Legal Protection of Trade Marks

(1) The following shall not be registered –
    (a) signs which do not satisfy the requirements of section 1(1),
    (b) trade marks which are devoid of any distinctive character,
    (c) trade marks which consist exclusively of signs or indications which may serve, in trade, to designate the kind, quality, quantity, intended purpose, value, geographical origin, the time of production of goods or of rendering of services, or other characteristics of goods or services,
    (d) trade marks which consist exclusively of signs or indications which have become customary in the current language or in the bona fide and established practices of the trade:
    Provided that, a trade mark shall not be refused registration by virtue of paragraph (b), (c) or (d) above if, before the date of application for registration, it has in fact acquired a distinctive character as a result of the use made of it.

KEY DEFINITION

Descriptive mark. A descriptive mark describes the goods or services in question and so cannot distinguish the goods or services of one trader from those of another, for it is applicable to all such goods.

The mark must not be *devoid* of distinctive character, meaning it must not be *wholly* descriptive such as 'Eurolamb' for lamb coming from Europe. It must have some aspect that will make it distinctive. In addition the mark must not be used to describe the quality or characteristics of the goods, for example 'best' or 'woolly', or to have become common in the relevant trade to describe the goods or services for which it is registered. This is intended to protect other traders who may honestly wish to use such marks in their own trade.

KEY DEFINITION

Distinctive mark. A mark that is distinctive is capable of distinguishing the goods of one trader from those of another.

You must note the caveat that if, although apparently lacking in distinctive character, the mark has acquired distinction through use it may be registered. It must still satisfy the requirement of section 1, of being capable of distinguishing. If it were a very common word, such as 'treat', it would be unlikely to succeed but if the public has been educated by prolonged advertising as in 'Have a break' used in relation to the chocolate bar KitKat, there may be a finding of distinction through use.

EXAM TIP

For the best marks in an essay you must demonstrate not just legal knowledge but an awareness of the reasons behind the legislation. Keep in mind that purely descriptive signs should not be monopolised by one undertaking but should be kept available for all traders to use. Descriptive marks will not be registered, despite the fact that defences may be available to honest traders who use such marks. Also remember that a sign may be made up of more than one aspect. As long as the descriptive part of the mark is not the most dominant part the additions may help it to acquire a distinctive character.

We are still left with the problem of whether a descriptive mark such as a geographical location can become distinctive through use.

KEY CASES

Windsurfing Chiemsee Productions v *Huber* [2000] Ch 523, ECJ

Concerning: Whether a geographical name can become distinctive through use

Facts

This was an application by a sportswear company situated near Lake Chiemsee to register the name Chiemsee which it had used for some time for its sportswear.

Legal principle

Geographical names are on the face of it unregistrable. They are descriptive and for public policy reasons they need to be kept available for all to use. However, if the name has acquired distinction as a mark through use, it is acceptable to register it as long as it is not being or is unlikely to be used in the future by other traders for that type of good or service.

Ilanah Simon, 'What's cooking at the CFI? More guidance on descriptive and non descriptive trademarks', [2003] EIPR 25(7) 322.

Explains the tension between Windsurfing and Baby Dry when using descriptive or laudatory terms. These cases conclude either that marks should not be registered if not viewed as a badge of origin or alternatively that there is a need to keep some trade marks available for the use of other traders.

Shape marks

KEY STATUTE

Section 3(2) Trade Marks Act 1994, Art 3 (1)(e) Directive on the Legal Protection of Trade Marks

'A sign shall not be registered as a trade mark if it consists exclusively of –
(a) the shape which results from the nature of the goods themselves,
(b) the shape of goods which is necessary to obtain a technical result, or
(c) the shape which gives substantial value to the goods'.

After distinctiveness and the rights of other traders to use common terms has been taken into account, other policy grounds can lead to a mark being rejected.

A shape mark must not result *exclusively* from the nature of the goods. Consequently one may not register the shape of a tyre. The shape must not be *necessary* to obtain a technical result even if there are other ways of obtaining that result, as in *Remington* (below). The shape must not give *substantial value* to the goods. So if you buy a good due to the shape of the mark rather than for the good itself this will be excluded. It is felt that if registration of such shapes were granted it would create a monopoly in those shapes and as a result a monopoly in the goods themselves. There is no exception to allow registration if the mark has become distinctive through use.

KEY CASE

***Koninklijke Philips Electronics* v *Remington Consumer Products Ltd* [2003] RPC 14, ECJ**

Concerning: The registrability of a functional shape mark

Facts

Philips sued for infringement of its pictorial trade mark which was in the shape of a three-headed rotary shaver. In response the validity of the mark was called into question as being an excluded functional shape.

Legal principle

The purpose of the provision is to prevent people obtaining exclusive rights over technical developments. Consequently the mark will not be registered even if there is another way of obtaining the end result. The test is – was it that shape due to its function?

To get a good mark you should show that you understand the consequence of a different decision. If the court had accepted that registration would be allowed for a shape mark with a technical function as long as there was another way of obtaining the same result, the provision would in effect have been made pointless. An unlimited monopoly would have been created over that way of doing something.

Bad faith

KEY STATUTE

Section 3(3)(a) and (b) and section 3(6) Trade Marks Act 1994, Art 3(1)(f) and (2)(d) Directive on the Legal Protection of Trade Marks

(3)   A trade mark shall not be registered if it is –
   (a) contrary to public policy or to accepted principles of morality, or
   (b) of such a nature as to deceive the public (for instance as to the nature, quality or geographical origin of the goods or service).
   . . .
(6)   A trade mark shall not be registered if or to the extent that the application is made in bad faith.

A mark will not be registered if it is contrary to public policy or to accepted principles of morality. However, keep in mind that public policy and the moral principles of right-thinking members of the public may change with time. Cases on this topic must be read in light of the morals of society at the time the case was heard.

A mark will not be registered if it is deceptive: for example, indicating an item is made of wool when it is in fact made of polyester or that it had been made in a particular location when it had not. A registration will also be denied if of a protected emblem or made in bad faith. Bad faith can have various meanings. Lack of intention to use the mark will show bad faith, as will attempting to register a mark to which it is known another is entitled. This could be to cash in on another's reputation or to prevent another trader from registering it.

KEY DEFINITION

Bad faith. Bad faith is behaviour falling short of acceptable standards of commercial behaviour.

Once the hurdles of the absolute grounds for refusal have been overcome, it is then time to consider other undertakings that may have marks which could be affected by the granting of a new trade mark.

Relative grounds for refusal

KEY STATUTE

Section 5(1) Trade Marks Act 1994, Art 4(1)(a) Directive on the Legal Protection of Trade Marks

'(1) A trade mark shall not be registered if it is identical with an earlier trade mark and the goods or services for which the trade mark is applied for are identical with the goods or services for which the earlier trade mark is protected.'

Identical signs may not be registered for identical goods. No confusion is required by the consumer for refusal of registration on these grounds. A sign will be held to be identical to a trade mark where it reproduces, without any modification or addition, all the elements constituting the trade mark or where, if viewed as a whole, it contains differences so insignificant that they may go unnoticed by an average consumer.

Average consumer

KEY DEFINITION

Average consumer. The average consumer is taken to be a consumer of the goods concerned who is reasonably well informed, reasonably observant and circumspect (careful).

KEY STATUTE

Section 5(2) Trade Marks Act 1994, Art 4(1)(b) Directive on the Legal Protection of Trade Marks

'(2) A trade mark shall not be registered if because –
(a) it is identical with an earlier trade mark and is to be registered for goods or services similar to those for which the earlier trade mark is protected, or
(b) it is similar to an earlier trade mark and is to be registered for goods or services identical with or similar to those for which the earlier trade mark is protected, there exists a likelihood of confusion on the part of the public, which includes the likelihood of association with the earlier trade mark.'

KEY DEFINITION

Similar goods or services. Goods or services are similar if they are in competition; if the consumer would buy one instead of the other.

A trade mark will not be registered if:

- the mark is either identical or similar to an earlier mark
- it is registered in relation to goods or services which are either similar or identical to the earlier mark
- *and* there is a likelihood of confusion on the part of the consumer.

REVISION NOTE

Go to Chapter 9 and make sure that you understand the connection between registrability and infringement.

How the likelihood of confusion is assessed

The likelihood of confusion must be appreciated globally. You must take into account the visual, aural and conceptual similarities of the marks. You must bear in mind their distinctive and dominant components. A lesser degree of similarity between the marks may be offset by a greater similarity between the goods (or services), and vice versa. There is a greater likelihood of confusion where the earlier trade mark has a highly distinctive character, either because it is a very unusual mark, or because it has become highly distinctive through use.

The average consumer normally perceives a mark as a whole and does not analyse its various details. It is the initial impact that counts. If the earlier mark is very distinctive either because it is very unusual or it has become very well known, consumers are likely to think of it on seeing a similar mark and become confused. However, you must also keep in mind the way the consumer perceives a mark. Are they likely to see it or hear it? Two marks when spoken may sound similar but if the consumer will only see the mark and not hear it spoken, it is the visual aspect you must consider and which must lead to confusion.

KEY CASE

Lloyd Schuhfabrik Meyer & Co GmbH v *Klisjen Handel BV* [2000] FSR 77, ECJ

Concerning: Confusion in relation to a trade mark

Facts

Lloyds was a mark for shoes which was distinctive through use, while Klijsen manufactured similar goods under the Loint's brand.

Legal principle

The more similar the goods and the more distinctive the earlier mark, the more likely there is to be confusion on the part of the consumer.

Problem area: Who must be confused and what must they be confused about?

Applying the tests of similarity, confusion, etc. to a given fact situation can be a challenge but it is wise to remain heedful that it is the consumer whose confusion must be established. Mere association is not sufficient unless this association leads to confusion. The consumer must believe that the goods came from the same or economically linked undertakings. It will help if you keep in mind that the basic function of a trade mark is an indicator of origin.

Trade marks of repute

KEY STATUTE

Section 5(3) Trade Marks Act 1994, Art 4(3) and (4)(a) Directive on the Legal Protection of Trade Marks

'(3) A trade mark which –
    (a) is identical with or similar to an earlier trade mark,
         shall not be registered if, or to the extent that, the earlier trade mark has a reputation in the United Kingdom (or, in the case of a Community trade mark or international trade mark (EC) in the European Community) and the use of the later mark without due cause would take unfair advantage of, or be detrimental to, the distinctive character or the repute of the earlier trade mark.'

In the past this provision related only to similar marks and non-similar goods. Due to the Trade Mark (Proof of Use, etc.) Regulations 2004 it also applies to similar marks and similar goods. There is no requirement for confusion in this provision but there must be some link made by the consumer between the two marks. The first thing that must be established in order to take advantage of this provision is that the earlier trademark has a reputation among a substantial part of the public in a significant part of the territory at issue.

KEY CASE

General Motors v *Yplon* [2000] RPC 572, ECJ

Concerning: Who must know of and how aware must they be of a trademark for it to be a mark with a reputation

Facts
General Motors was the proprietor of the mark 'Chevy' for motor vehicles who objected to Yplon registering the mark 'Chevy' for detergents and cleaning materials.

KEY CASE

Legal principle

The mark must have acquired a reputation with a substantial part of the relevant public in a significant part of the territory, but who the public are depends on the product. The market share, intensity of sale, geographical location and duration of use and the advertising of the mark must all be considered.

Once you have established that the mark has a reputation you must then prove that the mark is being used without due cause. There should be no overriding reason why the new mark must be used. It may also take unfair advantage of the mark with a reputation. That is use showing a disregard for the standards of acceptable commercial behaviour leading to increased sales of the new mark. Alternatively, use of the new mark may cause blurring, the lessening of the capacity of the famous mark to identify and distinguish goods, dilution which is the gradual whittling away of the identity of the mark in the mind of the public by its use on other goods, or tarnishment, detracting from the appeal of the existing mark, probably by some unsavoury connotation.

Chapter summary:
Putting it all together

Answer guidelines

See the problem question at the start of the chapter.

Points to remember when answering this question

▪ Explain that in order to register a trademark it must comply with the requirements of s1/art2 and s3/art3 and the sign must be capable of graphic representation and of distinguishing the goods of one undertaking from those of another undertaking.

▪ Advise as to whether the colour puce, applied to the type of good for which the mark is to be used, would be regarded as a badge of origin.

▪ The registration of smell and colour marks must be discussed with reference to the requirements laid out in *Shield Mark*. The mark must be clear, precise, self contained, easily accessible, intelligible, durable and objective. Here reference to an internationally recognised colour code such as Pantone would be expected. Ask, would a third party, when seeing the descriptions used, understand precisely what the mark was?

▪ Assess how likely it is that consumers will see the hedgehog shape as a badge of origin, the fundamental purpose of a trade mark, or whether they will merely regard it as the good itself.

▪ Shape marks which result from the nature of the goods and are necessary to obtain a technical result or give substantial value to the goods themselves are excluded from registration. These must be discussed with reference to *Philips* v *Remington* and the functional aspect of the shape of the toy.

Make your answer stand out

■ Point out that you are not tempted to fall into a trap. Show that you recognise that although a mark will not be registered if it is contrary to public policy, it must be the mark that causes the outrage, not the product. Here the purpose of the toy, anaesthetising children to sleep, may be distasteful but the effect of the gas is not the subject of registration.

FURTHER READING

Bainbridge, D.I. 'Smell, sound, colour and shape trade marks: an unhappy flirtation?' [2004] JBL 219.

Howell, C. 'Intel: a mark of distinction' [2007] 11 EIPR 441.

Walmsley, M. 'Too transparent? ECJ rules Dyson cannot register transparent collection chamber as a trade mark' [2007] 7 EIPR 298.

9
Trade mark infringement

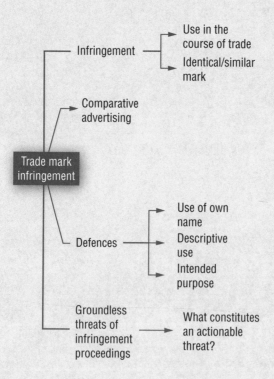

A printable version of this topic map is available from www.pearsoned.co.uk/lawexpress

Revision checklist

Essential points you should know:

- [ ] The meaning of an identical sign.
- [ ] Whether use of a trade mark must be in the course of trade.
- [ ] In what circumstances a trade mark can be used to compare one trader's goods or services with those of another.
- [ ] The limits of the own name defence.
- [ ] What will amount to descriptive use.
- [ ] When a registered trade mark may be used to indicate the intended purpose of another's goods or services.

Introduction

A trade mark gives the proprietor the exclusive right to use that mark in respect to the goods or services for which it has been registered.

Infringement can extend to the spoken use of words as well as to graphic representation. The relative grounds of refusal of registration and the acts that amount to infringement are very similar but infringement is concerned with the use of a sign, whereas the relative grounds for refusal are concerned with conflict with an earlier trade mark. Apart from case law on use of a sign in the course of trade or use of a sign in a trade mark sense, case law on the relative grounds for refusal is exchangeable and applicable to actions on infringement. An application to register a trade mark can be opposed on the basis of an earlier UK or Community Trade Mark (please refer to Chapter 8 for a discussion on these sections) but infringement under the Trade Marks Act 1994 can only relate to trade marks having effect in the UK.

Assessment advice

Essay questions

An essay question may well ask about the issues of use and the difference between use of a trade mark to describe a good or service and use in the trade mark sense.

Problem questions

Remember that a problem question on this topic could include problems of jurisdiction as well as infringement itself. You must also be careful to consider whether any defences might affect your answer.

Sample question

Could you answer this question? Below is a typical essay question that could arise on this topic. Guidelines on answering the question are included at the end of this chapter, whilst a sample problem question and guidance on tackling it can be found on the companion website.

ESSAY QUESTION

The 10th recital of the preamble to the Directive [89/104/EEC] states that the function of a trade mark is in particular to guarantee the trade mark as an indication of origin, and that protection is absolute in the case of identity between the mark and the sign and between the goods or services concerned and those for which the mark is registered.

Critically discuss this statement in the light of Arsenal Football Club v Reed *[2003] RPC 144.*

■ Infringement

Use in the course of the trade

KEY STATUTE

Section 10(1) Trade Marks Act 1994, Art 5(1)(a) Directive on the Legal Protection of Trade Marks

'A person infringes a registered trade mark if he uses in the course of trade a sign which is identical with the trade mark in relation to goods or services which are identical with those for which it is registered'.

When talking about infringement under the Trade Marks Act 1994 (TMA), remember that there must actually be use of the mark and the use complained of must be both use in the UK and use in the course of trade. Although not flagged up in either the TMA or the Directive there is an issue as to whether the use in question has to be 'trade mark use'. Does trade mark use mean any use in commerce, such as a photograph of a footballer in his football shirt with his team logo?

KEY CASE

Arsenal Football Club plc **v** *Matthew Reed* **[2003] RPC 144, ECJ**

Concerning: Whether the use of a sign as a badge of support or loyalty created a sufficient impression of a connection as to amount to infringement of a trade mark as 'trade mark use' indicating origin.

KEY CASE

Facts

Arsenal Football Club had registered the names 'Arsenal' and 'Gunners' along with the club emblems for goods such as scarves and sports clothing. Mr Reed, under a disclaimer pointing out that they were unlicensed, sold similar goods with the club's names and emblems attached. The club claimed trade mark infringement but Mr Reed retorted that he was not using the club's mark in a 'trade mark sense'.

Legal principle

The issue is not whether there has been trade mark use. What is at issue is whether the use of the mark created the impression to the consumer that there was a material link with the proprietor (any disclaimer may not have been seen post sale). Unchecked use of the mark by a third party which is not descriptive use is likely to damage the main function of the mark because it could no longer guarantee origin. The fact here that the mark was a badge of allegiance was irrelevant.

It would seem that the use needs to be in a form that indicates the origin of the goods or services or use which affects the interests of the proprietor of the mark in some other form.

EXAM TIP

You should deal with any question involving this issue by asking whether there is commercial use which undermines the proprietor's interest. To show that you have a good understanding of the whole topic you should point out that even if regarded as initially infringing, if the facts allow there may be a defence if the mark is being used descriptively: s11(2)(b), Art 6(1).

There is still academic debate in this area, however.

FURTHER THINKING

Nigel Parker, 'A raw deal for performers: Part 2 – Anti-piracy' [2006] 7 Ent LR 204.
    This article considers the cases of *Arsenal* v *Reed*, where the ECJ decided that 'trade mark use' was not an essential requirement for infringement to be found, and *R* v *Johnstone* [2003] WLR 1736 where 'trade mark use' was held to be essential to a finding of infringement, Lord Nicholls in *Johnstone* concluding that the retailer of bootleg recordings of the Bon Jovi pop group, a registered trademark, had not intended to use the name as a trade mark but only as a description of the goods. Consequently the bootleg recordings did not infringe. Nigel Parker points out that this conclusion 'flatly contradicts the decision in

Arsenal v *Reed'* where it was held that neither confusion nor 'trade mark use' are required in a case where a third party's use threatens a trade mark's essential distinctive functions, and that such diametrically opposed interpretations by the House of Lords are highly undesirable.

Identical/similar mark

In order to infringe another's mark for section 10(1) the defendant must be using an identical mark. Does this mean the mark must be exactly the same?

Problem area: Identical/similar mark

Although similar marks are not identical marks the ECJ has used the concept of imperfect recollection in determining whether an almost identical sign is identical to the registered trade mark. This creates a blurring between what is an identical sign, where no confusion need be proved, and what amounts to a similar sign where confusion must be established.

If a sign is identical to a registered mark and the goods or services for which it is being used are identical, no confusion on the part of the consumer need be proved. Infringement will have occurred. If there is mere similarity in the marks and in the goods or services, evidence of actual confusion on the part of the consumer is needed in order to prove infringement. It is therefore important to know whether marks are identical or similar so that you know whether or not you need to prove that confusion has occurred.

KEY DEFINITION

Identical and similar marks. The average, reasonably well informed, observant and circumspect customer assessing the mark globally may not notice the addition of a hyphen or an apostrophe, especially when they are apart, but would notice the inclusion of an extra word, if the word would not go unnoticed by the average consumer.

KEY CASE

LTJ Diffusion SA v *Sadas Vertbaudet SA* [2003] FSR 608, ECJ

Concerning: Meaning of identical mark

Facts

The claimant was a clothing company with the trade mark 'Arthur' in a distinctive handwritten form. The defendant sold children's clothing by mail order and applied for a Community Trade Mark 'Arthur et Félicie'. The claimant objected to the defendant's use of the mark and had opposed the CTM application.

KEY CASE

Legal principle

'. . . a sign is identical to a trade mark where it reproduces, without any modification or addition, all the elements constituting the trade mark or where, viewed as a whole, it contains differences so insignificant that they may go unnoticed by an average consumer'.

There may be a successful infringement action where there is incomplete identity of the mark and the goods or services but where there is a likelihood of confusion on the part of the consumer. If a mark has a reputation and there is an identical or similar sign and goods or services which are either similar or dissimilar there may be a finding of infringement without any confusion. There must however be some link made in the mind of the consumer and there must also be a finding of unfair advantage or damage to the repute of the mark. In addition, the defendant must have no justification of due cause for use of the mark with a reputation.

REVISION NOTE

Apart from the fact that the mark must be used in the UK the requirements of section 10 Art 5 and section 5 Art 4 are almost identical. Section 10 should therefore be read in conjunction with the discussion on section 5 which is found in Chapter 8.

Comparative advertising

Although not found in some other states of the European Union, honest and fair comparative advertising is permitted in the UK both under the TMA and in the light of the Comparative Advertising Directive 97/55.

KEY DEFINITION

Comparative advertising. Comparative advertising is the use of a competitor's trade mark to highlight the comparative advantage of one's own rival goods or services.

KEY STATUTE

Section 10(6) Trade Marks Act 1994

'Nothing in the preceding provisions of this section shall be construed as preventing the use of a registered trade mark by any person for the purpose of identifying goods or services as those of the proprietor or a licensee.

But any such use otherwise than in accordance with honest practices in industrial or commercial matters shall be treated as infringing the registered trade mark if the use without due cause takes unfair advantage of, or is detrimental to, the distinctive character or repute of the trade mark'.

From this section we can see that a trader may use what is undisputedly the trademark of a rival on identical goods or services. This use of a rival's mark is only allowed as long as the use made of the mark is not misleading and is in accordance with honest commercial practices.

Problem area: Does the use have to be necessary?

If a trader uses a competitor's sign in advertising in order to compare their goods or services when it is not necessary to use the sign in order to indicate whose products are being compared, does this amount to unfair prejudice?

KEY CASE

O2 Holdings v *Hutchison* C-533/06 ECJ

Concerning: Use of a similar version of a competitor's sign and whether the use of the sign must be indispensable

Facts

O2 owned the O2 mark in addition to a pictorial mark of clear blue iridescent bubbles which promoted an image of vitality. H3G, a competitor in price comparative advertising, used an image of depressed looking black and white bubbles. O2 felt that this distorted version was detrimental to the fresh image of its product, and claimed that the use of the bubbles image was unnecessary as H3G could have relied on the O2 sign in order to compare prices of the products.

Legal principle

The use of a similar rather than identical sign may identify a competitor's goods by implication for the purpose of the directive. Use of such a sign need not be indispensable as long as it meets the requirements for lawfulness.

There is an assumption that comparative advertising should be allowed. The fact that H3G could have compared the price of the goods using just the O2 mark rather than the bubbles was irrelevant. Use would be unlawful if the reputation of O2 was in some way associated with or hijacked by H3G or the distortion of the mark discredited or denigrated the O2 sign. It is up to the referring court to decide if such comparative advertising had in fact presented the O2 mark in a negative light.

■ Defences

Practical considerations are important when considering defending any alleged trademark infringement. A defendant must make sure that it is worth defending his actions. Establishing a defence could cost a great deal of money and may be unsuccessful. It may be more sensible to give an undertaking not to continue to use the sign.

KEY STATUTE

Section 11(2)(a) Trade Marks Act 1994, Art 6(1) Directive on the Legal Protection of Trade Marks

'A registered trade mark is not infringed by –

a) the use by a person of his own name and address,

b) the use of indications concerning the kind, quality, intended purpose value, geographical origin, the time of production of goods or rendering of services, or other characteristics of goods or services, or

c) the use of the trade mark where it is necessary to indicate the intended purpose of a product or service (in particular, as accessories or spare parts) provided the use is in accordance with honest practices in industrial or commercial matters.'

Use of own name

The provision states that as long as the use does not amount to passing off, the defence will apply to the use of a natural person's own name. It has also been accepted for full company names. It would seem therefore that there would be nothing to stop a person changing their name to that of a successful competitor and then pleading this defence. You must however ask yourself, would this be regarded as an honest practice?

KEY CASE

Asprey and Garrard Ltd v *WRA (Guns) Ltd* [2002] FSR 487, CA

Concerning: The use of a newly adopted company or trading name

Facts

A family business was sold along with the trade mark Aspreys but a member of the Asprey family and ex employee of the company then began to use his name as a trade name for similar luxury goods.

Legal principle

The 'own name' defence does not apply to the names of new companies or new trade names, as otherwise the route to piracy would be obvious.

Descriptive use

Some parts of this defence may on the face of it seem irrelevant. Section 3 Art 3 Directive should have prevented marks such as those which indicate the kind or quality of goods from being registered. If the mark however was not exclusively descriptive or it had acquired distinction through use, registration might have been allowed. This defence may then be needed to protect an honest trader who wishes to use such a word in his own business. There is a debate about whether some types of use are descriptive use, needed in order to let the consumer know the various characteristics of the goods, or infringing use.

REVISION NOTE

Please refer back to Chapter 8 for further discussion of the descriptive and distinctive issue.

KEY CASE

***Bravado Merchandising Services Ltd** v **Mainstream Publishing (Edinburgh) Ltd** [1996] FSR 205, CSOH*

Concerning: The use of a trade mark as a description of the goods

Facts

The name of the pop group 'Wet wet wet' had been registered as a trade mark. A book was written about the group and the name of the group was used in the title.

Legal principle

The defence is available when all the characterisations of infringement are present, not so that a mark can be used in a trade mark sense but for pure descriptive use which conveys features or characteristics of the product concerned.

EXAM TIP

Please note that the question whether the use is descriptive or as a trade mark will only need to be addressed if infringement has first been established. If you are dealing with a problem question and you have found infringement it is worth looking to see if there is anything in the facts you have been given to raise such a defence. The problem of whether the use is descriptive or as a trade mark may then need to be discussed. Remember that although detriment does not have to be proved, use must be in accordance with honest practices in industrial or commercial matters. Keep in mind that what is regarded as honest commercial practice may change over time.

Intended purpose

This defence to an infringement action facilitates free competition. A garage which repairs BMW cars needs to use the BMW logo to advertise the fact that it offers that service. This defence allows such necessary and honest use of the trade mark.

KEY CASE

Gillette Company v *LA-Laboratories Ltd Oy* [2005] FSR 808, ECJ

Concerning: Whether the use of the trade mark to indicate the intended purpose was 'necessary' and honest

Facts
Gillette Company had a registration for the trade marks 'Gillette' and 'Sensor' for razors. LA-Laboratories made razors and blades sold under the trade mark Parason Flexor, and sold blades with a sticker applied to their packaging which stated, 'All Parason, Flexor and Gillette Sensor handles are compatible with this blade'.

Legal principle
Use of the trade mark was *necessary* if it was the only way in practice to allow the public to understand the intended purpose for that product. However, the use must not give the impression that there is a commercial connection or reduce the trade mark's value by affecting its distinctive character or by denigrating the mark. Nor must the use indicate that it is replica of the product bearing the trade mark.

■ Groundless threats of infringement proceedings

Having infringement proceedings brought against a business can be very disruptive. It can involve an injunction, search and seizure orders and other such remedies. This gives a great deal of power to the claimant. This power can be abused, and to prevent this happening the 'groundless threats' procedure was incorporated into the Trade Marks Act 1994.

KEY DEFINITION

Goundless threat. No matter how ambiguous or indecisive, a communication will be regarded as a threat if understood by the ordinary recipient of the communication to be a threat to bring infringement proceedings.

Any person affected by a threat made without due cause can apply to the court and seek a declaration that the threat is unjustified, and an injunction to prevent further threats and damages. This is particularly useful to small retailers.

KEY STATUTE

Section 21 Trade Marks Act 1994

Any person aggrieved may bring proceedings for relief where there has been an unjustified threat to bring proceedings for infringement of a registered trade mark. The relief sought can be an injunction, damages or a declaration that the threats are unjustifiable. The mere notification that a trade mark is registered does not constitute a threat of proceedings. This section does not however apply to the importation of goods, where the mark has been applied to goods or their packaging, or to the supply of services under the mark.

What constitutes an actionable threat?

Problem area: What constitutes an unjustified threat?

A threat can be in a letter or it can be spoken. It may be express or implicit. Such threats are usually but not necessarily made by letter. Mere notification of the existence of the trade mark will not constitute a threat. If however a communication in whatever form is meant to unnerve the recipient or make them seriously think that what they are doing, if continued, may result in proceedings being brought, that will constitute a threat.

KEY CASE

L'Oreal (UK) Ltd v *Johnson & Johnson* [2000] FSR 686, ChD

Concerning: What amounts to a threat to bring proceedings

Facts

The claimants' solicitors wrote to the defendant asking whether infringement proceedings of the defendant's marks 'would be brought by reason of their use of similar words for similar products'. The letter in reply contained an enigmatic message but mentioned the possibility in the future of proceedings for infringement.

Legal principle

The test as to whether a communication amounted to a threat was whether it would be understood by the ordinary recipient in the position of the claimant as constituting a threat of proceedings for infringement.

Chapter summary:
Putting it all together

☐ Can you tick all the points from the revision checklist at the beginning of this chapter?

☐ Take the **end-of-chapter quiz** on the companion website.

☐ Test your knowledge of the cases below with the **revision flashcards** on the website.

☐ Attempt the essay question from the beginning of the chapter using the guidelines below.

☐ Go to the companion website to try out other questions.

Answer guidelines

See the essay question at the start of the chapter.

Points to remember when answering the question

▪ You have been asked to address a particular aspect of infringement so do not construct your answer in a way that is a summary of the whole topic.

▪ This question is concerned with s 10(1) and the use of an identical sign in relation to identical goods. There is no requirement of confusion so this does not need to be discussed. The focus should be upon the mark being used in the course of trade.

▪ There has been much debate about whether use in the course of trade must be use as a 'trade mark'. Briefly outline the issues.

▪ A comparison of the approaches taken by Laddie and the ECJ in *Arsenal* would be wise. Laddie J concentrated upon the perception of the consumer as to 'trade mark use' while the ECJ stated that whether there had been 'trade mark use' was not the appropriate question. The essential issue was whether the use made of the mark had affected the proprietor's interests, having regard to the trade mark's functions.

▪ The ECJ did not consider either the opinions of the consumer nor the infringer when deciding whether the proprietor's interests had been affected.

▪ Most descriptive use would not affect the proprietor's interest (*Bravado Merchandising*) but it would of course depend on the facts of each case.

Make your answer stand out

- This issue raises wider policy considerations such as a fear that intellectual property can create an unfair monopoly. Demonstrating an awareness of this will gain you a better mark, as will referring to the consequences of the different approaches to 'trade mark use' (see Further Reading) alluding to the uncertainty in this area created by the House of Lords in Johnstone.

FURTHER READING

Isaac, B. and Joshi, R. 'What does identical mean?' [2005] 5 EIPR 184.

Johnson, H. 'Comparative advertising: the battle of the bubbles – *02 Holdings Ltd* v *Hutchinson 3G Ltd* [2006] 2 Comms. L 51.

Simon, I. 'Nominative use and honest practices in industrial and commercial matters – a very European history' [2007] IPQ 117.

10
Passing off

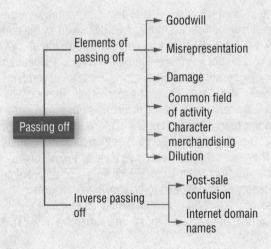

A printable version of this topic map is available from www.pearsoned.co.uk/lawexpress

Revision checklist

Essential points you should know:

- [ ] The meaning and ownership of goodwill.
- [ ] What amounts to misrepresentation.
- [ ] The difference between distinctive and descriptive.
- [ ] What constitutes damage and whether it is confined to buying the wrong goods.
- [ ] Whether the parties need to be engaged in trade.
- [ ] The meaning of a common field of activity and whether it is essential in all cases.
- [ ] What amounts to inverse passing off and whether post-sale confusion leads to passing off.
- [ ] Passing off and internet domain names.

Introduction

Nobody has any right to present his goods as the goods of somebody else. Passing off is a tort developed out of deceit. It can be described as the common law form of trade mark law but it is wider than trade mark law. Passing off can be used to prevent damage to not only distinctive names, numbers and devices but colours, the style of advertising campaigns, shapes and packaging. Passing off protects the property right in the goodwill of a business, not a mark itself. The goodwill is usually in the UK. Actual or likely damage, such as the diversion of business or damage to reputation, exposure to litigation or erosion of the mark, is a requirement for the commission of the tort. There must have been a false representation, intentional or unintentional, coming from the defendant, either verbally or by use of a name, get-up or logo which causes confusion in the mind of the customer or potential customer. The claimant's actual identity does not need to be known to consumers. It is generally accepted that regardless of the fact that customers may be misled, honest use of one's own name is permitted, but such use must not be made in a way that would exaggerate the connection.

Assessment advice

Essay questions

Passing off lends itself to essay questions. It is a tort that was created to encourage fairness and honesty amongst traders and it requires that the public be deceived [confused]. However, as the attributes of the public have changed over time, so too might the outcome of particular cases and this change can be analysed with reference to any policy issues or development in other areas of law such as trade marks.

Problem questions

It is important to identify all the issues raised in a problem question. But keep in mind that the basic requirements needed for a passing off action to succeed must all be present. Once you have identified the issues then apply the relevant authority to them and decide if you have indeed got what amounts to the tort of passing off, or if not, why not.

Sample question

Could you answer this question? Below is a typical problem question that could arise on this topic. Guidelines on answering the question are included at the end of this chapter, whilst a sample essay question and guidance on tackling it can be found on the companion website.

PROBLEM QUESTION

Two months ago Mr Raz took part in a popular TV programme where entrepreneurs attempt to gain investment from rich businessmen. Mr Raz won a substantial investment for his 'Koconut Sauce', a high quality tangy sauce to be used with savoury dishes marketed in a coconut-shaped plastic bottle. Mr Raz had created a song called 'I am a Koca-koca Nut' which he sang on the TV programme and which has since been used in an extensive advertising campaign to promote the sauce. An extended version of the advertisement has been released as a music video and has been a great success. The video features Mr Raz playing his guitar sitting under a coconut tree while surrounded by bottles of the sauce. The sauce is marketed in most supermarket chains.

Betty runs an organic burger bar called Betty's Burgers. The bar has a reputation for home-made produce. Betty has put up a large sign in her shop saying 'Put coconut sauce on your Betty Burger'. Betty has the video of Mr Raz as background music playing almost non-stop in her burger bar. She has registered the domain name coconutsauce.co.uk and has started taking orders online to supply organic food shops with her coconut sauce.

Advise Mr Raz as to whether he could bring a successful passing off action against Betty.

◼ The elements of passing off

The 'classical trinity' requirements for a finding of passing off are:

- ◼ the existence of the claimant's goodwill
- ◼ a misrepresentation as to the goods or services offered by the defendant, and
- ◼ damage (or likely damage) to the claimant's goodwill as a result of the defendant's misrepresentation.

KEY DEFINITION

Passing off. Passing off is an attempt by trader B to take advantage of the goodwill established by trader A, to the detriment of trader A.

Goodwill

KEY DEFINITION: GOODWILL

Goodwill is the attractive force attached to the name, get-up or logo which brings in custom.

Passing off does not protect the mark itself but the goodwill associated with the mark. In order to attract goodwill the mark, get-up or logo must be distinctive of the claimant's goods or services. Otherwise it would be impossible to show that goodwill was associated specifically with the claimant's mark rather than that of any other trader. On the face of it a descriptive word, get-up or logo is not distinctive and therefore is incapable of attracting goodwill. It may however become distinctive if used in an unusual or unexpected context or if it has become distinctive through exclusive use by the claimant.

KEY CASE

***Reckitt & Colman Products Ltd* v *Borden Inc* [1990] 1 ALL ER 873 (Jif Lemon case) HL**

Concerning: Use of a deceptively similar but descriptive 'get-up'

Facts

The claimant sold Jif lemon juice in a plastic lemon-coloured and lemon-shaped receptacle. The defendant sold lemon juice in a similar but not identical container.

Legal principle

Although each case in passing off depends on its own particular facts, the existence of the claimant's extensive and exclusive goodwill built up over many years, a misrepresentation as to the goods or services offered by the defendant, and damage (or likely damage) to the claimant's goodwill as a result of the defendant's misrepresentation amounted to passing off.

Although the Jif Lemon case is authority for the 'classical trinity' of goodwill, misrepresentation and damage the 'Advocaat' case is a second source of the basic requirements for success in a passing off action. This case demands a misrepresentation made by a trader in the course of trade to prospective or ultimate customers of goods or services supplied by him which is calculated to injure the business or goodwill of another trader and which causes actual damage. This case also raised an issue as to whether consumers had to be deceived into buying the wrong goods or services or whether dilution or erosion amounted to passing off.

Erven Warnink Besloten Vennootschap v *J Townend & Sons Ltd* [1979] AC 731 (Advocaat case) HL

Concerning: Whether passing off could result even if consumers did not mistakenly buy the wrong goods

Facts

Substantial loss of sales was suffered by a well-known and popular liqueur called Advocaat due to a similar but cheaper and inferior-quality drink called 'Keeling's Old English Advocaat' being placed on the market.

Legal principle

Not only damage due to lost sales but damage to reputation by being associated with an inferior product amounted to passing off and traders either individually or as a class could be protected from deceptive use of their name by competitors.

Reputation is not the same as goodwill. A trader can have a reputation but carry out no business in this country. Traditionally there must be some business or market in the UK for goodwill to exist. The time taken to develop goodwill and the extent of the area affected are fact dependant, as is the ownership of the goodwill itself. Goodwill, the ability to pull in customers, is of value because of its power to promote future businesses. The acquisition and durability of goodwill is an area of law that develops as business practices change. With greater advertising and globalisation goodwill can spread faster and wider in the future, but for passing off there must still be goodwill rather than a mere reputation.

Scandecor Development AB v *Scandecor Marketing AB* [1998] FSR 500, HL

Concerning: Whether a parent or subsidiary company owns the goodwill in a name

Facts

A Swedish poster-producing company was split and set up a UK subsidiary trading under the name Scandecor which was the sole retailer in the UK. The UK company continued to obtain its posters from the Swedish company.

Legal principle

The goodwill belongs to the company that either traded or exercised business control over activities in the UK.

Misrepresentation

KEY DEFINITION

Misrepresentation. A misrepresentation is a false description made consciously or unconsciously by the defendant. Such representation can be implied by the use of a mark, trade name or get-up with which the goods of the claimant are associated in the minds of a substantial number of ordinary sensible members of the public who have been or are likely to be misled due to the representation.

Deception due to misrepresentation is an essential element for a finding of passing off. Merely demonstrating that as a result of the similarities between two marks people may be confused does not mean there is passing off.

Arsenal Football Club plc v *Reed* [2001] RPC 922, ChD

Concerning: Use of identical marks on identical goods

Facts

The defendant had, for over 30 years, sold memorabilia bearing the football club's name and logo. However, due to a disclaimer the defendant's customers realised that the goods neither came from nor were sanctioned by the club. They bought his products as badges of allegiance to the football club.

The disclaimer Mr Reed displayed here was sufficient to prevent the misrepresentation necessary for passing off; it was however insufficient to prevent consumers making a material link when the case was referred to the ECJ on the trade mark infringement issue.

Legal principle

For passing off to have occurred customers or ultimate consumers must have been deceived with a real likelihood of confusion.

EXAM TIP

Although many of the concepts used in the trade marks statutes are similar to those found in passing off, the two are distinct. You must make sure that you do not combine them together in your discussions. You may find that an examination question may contain issues that relate to both passing off and trade marks but you must keep these issues separate and deal with them independently.

Damage

Diversion of business, damage to reputation, exposure to litigation or erosion of the mark can all amount to damage.

Taittinger SA v *Allbev Ltd* [1993] FSR 641, CA

Concerning: Whether 'extended' passing off can be found due to erosion of goodwill even when there is no confusion in the mind of the consumer

Facts

The defendant, an English company, made a cheap non-alcoholic drink called Elderflower Champagne and although no confusion was alleged the growers of the sparkling wine objected to the use of the word Champagne.

Legal principle

Erosion of the distinctiveness of the name with a reputation is an actionable form of damage to the goodwill of the business of the claimant.

Common field of activity

A common field of activity is no longer an essential requirement of passing off. However, lack of some similarity in the field creates a presumption that confusion and therefore passing off has not occurred. The public are unlikely to make a connection and be misled in the absence of a common field of activity unless the goods or services are in effect household names.

Character merchandising

Problem area: Character merchandising

Character merchandising is the licensing of mainly fictional characters. If goodwill has been established in the character and the name is used by another trader, passing off could arise. However, a lack of a common field of activity can present a problem with such character merchandising. Use of the name Wombles for rubbish skips was held not to be passing off because it did not compete with the owner of the name who traded in licensing children's TV characters.

There have been developments in this area. They are however confined to circumstances where the public can be shown to be conscious of merchandising in the particular field. This awareness will make them more likely to mistakenly assume that there has been a licence or sponsoring agreement entered into for the use of a personality's name or image. For other character merchandising, where no such assumption is likely to be made, it is still unlikely that a passing off action will succeed.

KEY CASE

Irvine v *Talksport Ltd* [2003] FSR 619, Ch D

Concerning: Whether falsely implying that a celebrity has endorsed a product is actionable under passing off

Facts

The defendant ran the radio station 'Talk Radio'. They used a doctored photograph of Eddie Irvine, the Formula One Grand Prix racing driver, in a promotional campaign having substituted a portable radio clearly displaying the words 'Talk Radio' for a mobile phone.

Legal principle

Celebrities may have a proprietary right in the goodwill of their names or image and that right can be protected by bringing an action in passing off. Despite there being no common field of activity the public may nevertheless falsely assume that the product had been endorsed.

FURTHER THINKING

Gary Scanlan, 'Personality, endorsement and everything – the modern law of passing off' [2003] 12 EIPR 563.

Until *Irvine* v *Talksport* the requirement of a common field of activity has traditionally been a barrier to celebrities using passing off to prevent their name or image being used by others. The Scanlan article here criticises the extension of passing off as in effect having no authority, claiming that what the courts appear to be doing is creating a 'personality right' and that monopolies of this type should not be created for policy reasons.

Inverse passing off

KEY DEFINITION

Inverse passing off. Inverse passing off occurs where the defendant falsely claims that the claimant's goods or services are actually made or provided by the defendant.

Inverse passing off is the opposite of traditional passing off where trader B tries to take the customers of trader A by pretending that his goods are the goods of trader A. With inverse passing off trader B pretends that trader A's goods are in fact trader B's. There can be no lost sales due to buyers confusing the defendant's products (or services) with those of the claimant, but there can be damage to trader A if the defendant's product is inferior to the claimant's product and buyers mistakenly think that the defendant's product is that of the claimant.

KEY CASE

Bristol Conservatories Ltd v *Conservatories Custom Built Ltd* **[1989] RPC 455, CA**

Concerning: Inverse passing off

Facts

The defendant's sales representatives showed potential customers photographs of conservatories as a sample of the defendant's workmanship. The photographs were, in fact, of the claimant's conservatories.

Legal principle

This misdescription harmed the claimant's goodwill and constituted passing off.

Post-sale confusion

> ## KEY DEFINITION
>
> **Post-sale confusion.** Post-sale confusion is where the misrepresentation comes after the goods have been purchased.

Even if there is no deception at the time of sale, later confusion as to the origin of the name, mark or device can still damage the goodwill by a process of dilution or erosion. Although UK cases have not regarded post-sale confusion as amounting to passing off there has been an extension of passing off in other jurisdictions (see *Levi Strauss & Co* v *Kimbyr Investments Ltd.*, [1994] FSR 335).

Bostick Ltd v Sellotape GB Ltd [1994] RPC 556, ChD

Concerning: Whether a get-up which could only be seen post sale could lead to passing off due to erosion of goodwill

Facts

The claimant sold blue adhesive putty called 'Blu-tack' and the defendant sold a similar blue product called 'Sellotak' but the blue could only be seen after purchase and removal from its packaging.

Legal principle

As the defendant's product could not be seen at the point of sale, there was no danger of confusion.

Passing off and internet domain names

Although not the typical application of passing off it has been successfully pleaded concerning the wrongful use of domain names. If a third party without due cause registers company A's trading name as a domain name, this will prevent company A from registering the name itself and will constitute damage to company A. Such 'Cybersquatting' cases have usually included an offer to sell the domain name to company A for an inflated price.

Marks & Spencer plc v *One in a Million Ltd* [1998] FSR 265, CA

Concerning: Whether registering as a domain name the name of another's company with associated goodwill constituted passing off

Facts

The defendants had registered a number of names including 'bt.org' but had not made any use of the domain names in the course of trade.

Legal principle

It was sufficient for passing off for a person to put an 'instrument of deception' into the hands of another or to authorise another to do so.

For such an action to succeed there must still be proof of damage or a likelihood of damage and this will be difficult to show if the claimant has chosen a descriptive or generic name for his business such as Radio Taxis for a taxi cab business.

REVISION NOTE

It is important to remember that passing off can be used in conjunction with trade mark infringement or where for some reason a trade mark application has not been made or a trade mark has been lost. Please refer to Chapters 8 and 9 on these aspects of trade marks.

Chapter summary:
Putting it all together

☐ Can you tick all the points from the revision checklist at the beginning of this chapter?

☐ Take the **end-of-chapter quiz** on the companion website.

☐ Test your knowledge of the cases below with the **revision flashcards** on the website.

☐ Attempt the problem question from the beginning of the chapter using the guidelines below.

☐ Go to the companion website to try out other questions.

Answer guidelines

See the problem question at the start of the chapter.

Points to remember when answering this question

■ To begin with you must identify the relevant issues to establish whether Mr Raz has goodwill in his name, mark or get-up. You must then determine whether there has been a misrepresentation and what damage may have ensued.

■ Two months is a relatively short time to establish goodwill but the publicity surrounding his TV appearance would help to establish it.

■ His goodwill would be attached to the name, get-up and the song but are they distinctive enough to be protected?

■ The name of the sauce. Koconut spelt with a K is not totally descriptive but would this K be obvious to the average consumer?

■ The shape of the bottle is part of the get-up but is it too descriptive?

■ Would the distinctive spelling of the sauce be recognised in the song which would be heard rather than seen?

■ Will the customers have been deceived (confused) by any misrepresentation?

■ Look at the use made of the sauce, on all savoury dishes in comparison to burgers only. Is there a common field of activity?

■ The Koconut sauce is sold in supermarkets but not Betty's Bar so would there be confusion at point of sale?

■ Betty's Burger Bar has a reputation for home-made produce.

■ The spelling of her sauce is purely descriptive.

■ Customers will see the spelling in a written form rather than hear it sung.

■ Betty is serving the sauce in her bar and selling via the internet rather than in a supermarket.

■ She has registered the domain name but is using it in the furtherance of her own business rather than as an instrument of deception.

■ What damage do you think Mr Raz has suffered or could suffer? Damage does not have to be lost sales but could be damage to reputation or even exposure to litigation. (Health and safety is important with food.)

Make your answer stand out

■ Make your reader aware that passing off cannot be used to prevent competition. It can be used only to prevent the use of another's goodwill to their detriment.

FURTHER READING

Harrold, L. 'Beyond the well-trodden paths of passing off: the High Court decision in *L'Oreal* v *Bellure*, [2006] 5 EIPR 304.

Moscona, R. 'The sale of business goodwill and the seller's right to use his own name' [2006] 2 EIPR 106.

Sims, A. 'Rethinking one in a million' [2004] 10 EIPR 442.

And finally, before the exam. . .

☐ Look at the summary checklist of the points below. Are you happy that you can now tick them all? If not, go back to the particular chapter and work through the material again. If you are still struggling, **seek help** from your tutor.

☐ Go to the companion website and revisit the interactive **quizzes** provided for each chapter.

☐ Make sure you can recall the **legal principles** of the key cases and statutes which you have revised.

☐ Go to the companion website and test your knowledge of cases and terms with the **revision flashcards.**

☐ Make sure you understand the European Community aspect of the IP issues studied on your course.

Make sure that before the examination you can explain:

▪ What is duration, original, qualifying and fixation and the difference between secondary and derivative works in copyright.

▪ What are joint authorship, employee-created works and moral rights?

▪ What are beneficial ownership, implied licences, altered copying, and communication to the public?

▪ What are the defences, permitted acts, remedies and secondary infringements?

▪ Who is bound by confidentiality, what is the position of employees and what is the public interest defence?

▪ What are novelty, enabling disclosure, inventive step and industrial application, and how is the scope of an invention determined in a patent application?

▪ What is a variant infringement, and when is knowledge required?

▪ What is the reader skilled in the art and what are the defences and remedies for patent infringement?

▪ What are the rules for subsistence: the differences between Community and UK designs, a product, complex product, novelty and individual character?

- Can you describe the informed user, immaterial difference, commonplace, the must-fit/match exceptions and infringement?
- What is a sign and graphical representation for trade mark purposes?
- What are the absolute and relative grounds for refusal of registration and identical/similar marks/goods?
- What is a consumer, how will they perceive signs/goods and how is likelihood of confusion assessed?
- What are having a reputation, without due cause, unfair advantage and detriment?
- Must a trade mark be used in the course of trade?
- When can another's mark be used comparatively and what is the own name defence?
- What is descriptive use, and when can a mark be used to indicate the intended purpose of another's goods?
- What are goodwill, misrepresentation and damage in relation to passing off?
- Is engagement in trade necessary, and what is a common field of activity?
- What are inverse passing off, post-sales confusion and cybersquatting?

By using this revision guide to supplement your work during the module and the other materials you have been directed to by your module lecturer, you should now have a good knowledge and understanding of intellectual property law and how the individual rights work, whether alone or together. You should also be well prepared for examination questions, whether set as essay questions or problem questions.

Linking it all up

Check where there are overlaps between subject areas. Make careful notes of these as a knowledge of how one topic can lead into another can increase your marks significantly. Here are some examples:

- There is an overlap between artistic copyright, especially artistic craftsmanship and design right.
- The public interest defence is relevant to copyright and as a defence to a breach of confidence.
- Confidentiality is important in the pre-filing stage of a patent application.

ESSAY/ PROBLEM QUESTION

Imagine a mobile phone. Describe in detail the intellectual property rights that could be connected with that phone.

Answer guidelines

Points to remember when answering this querstion

■ Patent could protect new and inventive parts of the phone or the process used in manufacturing.

■ Confidentiality may arise in the pre-filing period. If disclosed, not in confidence, novelty may be lost and no patent will be granted.

■ The shape of the phone if new and distinctive may be protected by either UK or Community design right.

■ Copyright may exist in the ring-tone. Moral rights may belong to the author if appropriately asserted but there may be an exception for this use. Copyright protection may exist for manuals that accompany the phone, being the property of the writer unless created in the course of employment.

■ The names, logos or jingles used may have been registered as trademarks.

Make your answer stand out

■ By commenting on any possible licensing arrangement and attempts made by some proprietors such as Remington to extend patent protection via design, copyright or trade mark law.

Glossary

Key definitions

Authorise
In relation to copyright infringement authorise means the grant or purported grant to a third person of the right to do the act complained of

Average consumer
For trade marks, the average consumer is taken to be a consumer of the goods concerned who is reasonably well informed, reasonably observant and circumspect

Bad faith
In relation to trade marks, bad faith is behaviour falling short of acceptable standards of commercial behaviour

Commonplace
Definitions include:
'... any design which is trite, trivial, common-or-garden, hackneyed or of the type which would excite no peculiar attention in those in the relevant art is likely to be commonplace'
'What really matters is what prior designs the experts are able to identify and how much those designs are shown to be current in the thinking of designers in the field at the time of creation of the design in question'

Community design
A community design has a unitary character and has equal effect throughout the Community: it may only be registered, transferred, surrendered, declared invalid or its use prohibited in relation to the entire Community

Comparative advertising
The use of a competitor's trade mark to highlight the comparative advantage of one's own rival goods or services

Descriptive mark
A descriptive mark describes the goods or services in question and so cannot distinguish the goods or services of one trader from those of another for it is applicable to all such goods

Distinctive mark
A mark that is distinctive is capable of distinguishing the goods of one trader from those of another

Goodwill
Goodwill is the attractive force attached to the name, get-up or logo which brings in custom

Groundless threats	No matter how ambiguous or indecisive, a communication will be regarded as a threat if understood by the ordinary recipient of the communication to be a threat to bring infringement proceedings
Identical and similar marks	The average, reasonably well informed, observant and circumspect customer assessing the mark globally may not notice the addition of a hyphen or an apostrophe, especially when they are apart, but would notice the inclusion of an extra word, if the word would not go unnoticed by the average consumer
Infringement	Infringement occurs if a validly patented product or process is exploited within the UK without the patentee's consent and with no defence available
Injunction	An order of the court which prohibits the commencement or continuance of an act or requires a person to perform an act
Inverse passing off	Inverse passing off occurs where the defendant falsely claims that the climant's goods or services are actually made or provided by the defendant
Joint/co-authorship	A work is a work of joint authorship if it is a collaborative work where the contribution of each of the authors is not distinct
Misrepresentation	A misrepresentation is a false description made consciously or unconsciously by the defendant. Such representation can be implied by the use of a mark, trade name or get-up with which the goods of the claimant are associated in the minds of a substantial number of ordinary sensible members of the public who have been or are likely to be misled due to the misrepresentation
Original	A work is original for copyright purposes if it has originated from the author and has not been copied for another work (note that for computer programs and databases, the work is original only if it is the author's own intellectual creation)
Passing off	Passing off is an attempt by trader B to take advantage of the goodwill established by trader A, to the detriment of trader A.
Post-sale confusion	Post-sale confusion is where the misrepresentation comes after the goods have been purchased
Private information	Information or conduct, the disclosure of which would be highly offensive to a reasonable person of ordinary sensibilities
Purposive approach	The purposive approach looks at the purpose or reason for making the claim
Similar goods or services	Goods or services are similar if they are in competition; if the consumer would buy one instead of the other

Person skilled in the art	An unimaginative person; or team of uninventive people, with the common general knowledge available to a person in the field at the date of filing, who will only think the obvious and will not question general assumptions
Trade marks – fundamental attributes	A mark will only be registered as a trademark if it is a sign, if it can be represented graphically and if it is capable of distinguishing one trader's goods or services from those of another
Trade secret	A trade secret is information that would cause real harm if it were disclosed to a competitor and the owner had limited the dissemination of the information

Other useful terms

Artists' resale right	The right of an author of an artistic work to a royalty on subsequent public resale of his work
Assignment	Transfer of ownership of an intellectual property right, such as copyright or a patent
Author	Generally, for the original works of copyright, the author is the person who creates it
Beneficial ownership	This applies typically to overcome a failure to properly provide for ownership, for example, by means of an express assignment of a right, so that the person who has paid for the creation of a work is given the right to use it under equity notwithstanding that the creator remains the owner at law
European Economic Area (EEA)	The Member States of the EC, Iceland, Liechtenstein and Norway
Exhaustion of rights	The owner of an intellectual property right which relates to goods or articles which have been put into circulation by him or with his consent anywhere within the European Economic Area cannot exercise that right to prevent the subsequent import, export or sale of those particular goods or articles and his right is said to be exhausted
Informed user	For design law, the informed user has experience of similar products and will be reasonably discriminatory and able to appreciate sufficient detail to decide whether or not the design under consideration creates a different overall impression, taking account of the degree of design freedom, if any
Permitted acts	Acts expressly permitted under the Copyright, Designs and Patents Act 1988 in relation to a copyright work that might otherwise infringe the copyright

Priority date	The date of filing a patent application or the date of filing an application for the same invention elsewhere during the previous 12 months and for which priority is claimed by the applicant
Royalty	A payment mechanism to allow another person or persons to exploit an intellectual property right, normally calculated on a percentage of the income derived from sales of works, goods or articles subject to the right
State of the art	In relation to an invention, it means all matter made available to the public at its priority date by means of written or oral description, by use or in any other way, whether in the UK or elsewhere

Further reading

If you are in doubt as to any legal terminology, you would be advised to consult one of the many comprehensive legal dictionaries available. Your institution's library is certain to have a good selection of these. Be wary of online dictionaries as the quality may vary. Suitable examples of legal dictionaries include:

FURTHER READING

Curzon, L. B. and Richards, P. (2007) *The Longman Dictionary of Law*, 7th edition, London: Longman.

Penner, J. E., Mozley, H. N. and Whiteley, G. C. (2001) *Mozley and Whiteley's Law Dictionary*, 12th edition, London: Lexis Nexis.

Woodley, M. (2005) *Osborn's Concise Law Dictionary*, 10th edition, Andover: Sweet & Maxwell.

For a wealth of material on intellectual property and with numerous links to useful websites, visit the UK Intellectual Property Office website at: http://www.ipo.gov.uk/

Index